MW01248900

THE ENEMY

Annie Anderson

Diligence Publishing Company
Bloomfield, New Jersey

The Scripture in this book is from the King James Version of the Bible.

THE ENEMY

Copyright © 2015
Annie Anderson
Diligence Publishing Company
Bloomfield, New Jersey
www.dpc-books.com
All Rights Reserved

No part of this book may be reproduced in any form without the written permission from the author except for brief passages included in a review.

To contact Annie Anderson to preach or speak at your church, organization, seminar or conference call (908) 343-9599 or email
andersonannie14@yahoo.com
montaguelee77@gmail.com

THE ENEMY

ISBN: 978-09963833-1-8

Printed in the United States

TABLE OF CONTENTS

ACKNOWLEDGEMENTS

To My Saviour,

Most important my sincere gratitude to Jesus Christ, my Lord and Saviour, who let me see myself. He saved me and gave me an understanding heart about salvation and what time of days we are living in. He has done marvelous things in my life whereof I'm glad about it. How can words adequately acknowledge all you have done for my family and me; Not only for my family and me but for the whole world. I love you Jesus more than I am able to express. I thank God for giving you to bail me out of my mess. I want to thank you for your longsuffering and your grace. I don't deserve any of it and I see the love you have shown toward us all. "Thank You Jesus."

My deepest appreciation to,

My family, for the hours I spent writing this book, how encouraging words came from them letting me know I could do it. The Lord saved every one of my sisters and brothers. Before my Mother went home to be with the Lord, she told us to "Stay with the Lord and keep the love for one another, and do all you can to help one another." When I think of my family, I think of Philippians 4:13 *"I can do all things through Christ which strengtheneth me."*

Two great nieces,

I have many great nieces, but these two I am with them most of the time. Zhanaye' L. Brown and La'Nayzha R. Washington (my prayer partner). They are my joy, the Bible says in Proverbs 22:6: *Train up a child in the way he should go: and when he is old, he will not depart from it.* They are in training, not only praying but they know how to praise God, sing for the Lord, and stand up and say "I Thank the Lord for being here." When it's time for the Word of God they get their Bibles. During Sunday School, they have their part in leading us into The Lord's Prayer and receiving the offering.

My Mother,

The late Mother Lillie Rebecca Person Taylor, I thank God for her birthing me. My life drew her and my family to Christ. God gave her ten years saved in this life, where she did a quick work for the Lord, and then He called her home.

Sister Dawn Clyburn,

I saw her grow up into the ministries, always planting her seeds to support the works of God. When you tell her the vision God has placed in your heart in doing a work for Christ, she's there to plant her seed of faith, and by her being a blessing to the works of Christ. The Lord has blessed her abundantly. I thank God for her.

To: All Pastors of God,

Living according to The Word of God, that love souls, teaching them the way of salvation and how to keep what they have in Christ Jesus.

To a Special Brother in Christ,

Bro. Kevin Davis, who is praying for me as I write. We used to do outreach ministry together, nursing homes, personal witness, and revival meetings. I got appointed into another field of experience that caused me to write.

To My Church Family,

True Vine Deliverance Ministries, thanks to everyone that prayed and supported me in the hours when I had to stop and go to God in prayer for myself. One time everything was at a stand still, I had to rebuke the enemy for trying to mess with my mind, telling me "You doing too much." While writing I let one year pass by me then a stop and start, one to three months of stopping again, then starting back writing. I had to go to God, you just don't know like I know, at that time I really needed God. I had to fast and pray about this book. I have seen bad days, in the afternoon I spend time writing, but most of my writing would be at night. The enemy fought with me big time so every week end after Friday service we would stay in the Church praying around the clock with fasting. That was a great help. Sometimes I would bring my pad there to write in between prayer. In fact, I finished my book at the church. When it was time to go home I wasn't ready to go. It's something how prayer works.

To Pastor Rebecca Simmons,

I thank God for your editing skills. You understood and you worked hard with me. You believe in what my book is all about. Every week you spent quality time with me and gave words of encouragement along with prayer. I could not have done it without you and your staff at Diligence Publishing Company. Thanks for your support of my book and for your wonderful professional service along with patience.

CHAPTER 1

MY LIFE

I would never have expected to write a book about the enemy, but when I think about my life, what I've been through and where the Lord has brought me from, um! I know there's an enemy somewhere. With this in my mind one day, my hands began to write. I didn't quite understand it, but as the years passed, I began to understand me. I have seen a lot of things happening in life. I have not been a lot of places, so I've seen things mostly in the Church, where some people are saved, many people are trying to get their lives together because of their lifestyle, and then you have those who act saved but are not.

I was born in a little town called Henderson, in the state of North Carolina, to my parents David and Lillie Rebecca Person Montague. I remember when our family lived with my daddy's sister; we call her aunt Fannie, she loved to go to church, worked in the church and kept us in church. I never knew that she ever claimed salvation, all I know is she loved to go to church. When I was about the age of 13, I remember we moved to another part of town. That section is called Mobile. We stayed on Nicholas Street. I went to church with this mother that lived across the street from us. I loved to go to church. I didn't really understand all that was going on, but I knew it was a good thing to do.

Later on in life, I stopped going to church. I got involved in other things that led me the wrong way. I started drinking strong drinks, fighting, and acting crazy. I almost got killed twice. I was in a bad car accident; my face by my eye was cut open. I went to the emergency room where they sewed the wounds up and the next two days I couldn't see so I had to be hospitalized. The doctors and nurses worked all night long on my face and eyes so I wouldn't get infected. I recovered from that. Now the next death – a gun was pointed to my head. God was so merciful to me. Someone called the police and a little before they got there the person that had the gun dropped it and ran. That night, the gun was pointed at my head, but the trigger was not pulled. Thank You Jesus!

I married very young, but was pregnant by another man. I lost the baby that I was carrying due to it being a tubal pregnancy. I didn't know what was wrong with me. I was in great pain and went to the emergency room every other day. They didn't know what was wrong with me. They just gave me pain pills and sent me home.

It came to a point where I went back to the hospital, and they kept me in the emergency room. For over three hours, I was in great pain and the way I felt I didn't care if I saw tomorrow. I asked the Lord *"Please make this pain go away."* This hospital didn't have the equipment that's available today in telling you your problem. Finally, they found the problem, and they rushed me to an emergency operation.

The doctor told me if I would have waited a few minutes longer I would have died. He said by the time they cut me open, the tube where the baby was had burst open, and there was blood everywhere. He said it was as if someone had shot me and the bullet fragments spread. I lost about four pints of blood and they gave me blood – a transfusion. Thank God the blood was not like it is now.

CHAPTER 2

GOD'S IN THIS PLAN

After all of that, I began to think about my life. Things were not looking good for me. I ended up back in the hospital in the middle of March 1973 for another operation; the Lord again brought me through. While in recovery, I prayed that God would show me a better way. It's funny how when we are in trouble, we always call on the Lord or pray to Him. Sometimes when the Lord helps us out, we go the other way until we need Him again; and we all are guilty of that.

God answered my prayers. I remember going to a healing service one night. Along with others, I was called out by this man of God to come forward. He told me exactly what was wrong with me. He said that God was going to heal me and that night God was going to visit me, and I wouldn't be no more the same. He said God called me for His service. To me, I felt like I was trapped in the arms of Jesus especially when I had prayed to Him early to show me a better way. In life God is working things out for our good, but we don't see it because we are trying to do things our way. I know He was working things out for me, but at that time I didn't see it.

As I left the service, I began to think. Days, weeks, months, and a year passed. I decided to run from God. I left New Jersey and went to Florida for all of the winter months. It seemed as though I had no rest or peace, and people were picking on me. Yes I had some really bad days, but this time seemed as though I was just unhappy and scared, The Lord was in the plan. He was dealing with me. I said within myself, *"I want to go back to New Jersey."* I knew then that running from God wouldn't work.

The time came for me to return to New Jersey. When I returned, I kissed the ground because I was glad to be back. My situation was the same, no rest or peace. Have you ever shut yourself off and decided not to come out? Well I did. I was inside the house drinking, playing my music and scared to come outside. Once again I was asking God to show me a better way than this. I didn't know Jesus, but I was praying to Him the same prayer each and every day.

My friend named Evelyn – we used to hang at her dad's auto body shop. We drank, laughed, and thought we were having a good time. One evening, her friends that once lived in New Jersey came back to visit. We got together, and we all had glasses. One of us poured into each glass some Scotch liquor. We toasted, and began to drink. When I turned the glass to my mouth and began to drink, I felt a hand that hit my hand that was holding the glass and knocked it right out of my hand. It hit the car glass where I was standing and hit the ground and broke. That scared me greatly – I was no more good. Not only that, but I was drinking it without it being mixed with anything – just straight Scotch liquor. Maybe I would have died. I don't know, but God knows and He came to my rescue.

Fear began to set in. I got house bound and didn't go out of the house. I was in a bad situation and couldn't help myself at all. Now I was in a place where I was scared, afraid to walk the street; it didn't matter what time it was, daytime, evening time or nighttime. God was dealing with me trying to get my attention, but I was slow of understanding what was going on.

My friend, Evelyn went out one night with one of her friends, Mary. I babysat that night for Evelyn. I had no idea where she was going. But she came home about three hours later and her whole face was lit up. She told me that they went to this church on the highway, and the Lord touched her.

She was so excited, saying the same thing over and over again, "You don't believe me?"

I told her, "Yes I do, since I was raised in church." I asked her the name of the church, and she told me. I told her "I'm planning to go to that church." So during the week in my planning on going to church that Sunday morning, the enemy used this person who I know but not as well, she's only my friend's babysitter. The whole week her father let her work in the store, where they sell wine, beer and liquor. She told me that I could come and get anything I want. I was thinking about getting my life together and the enemy was trying to stop me. I didn't know at that time so I went to the store. She said I could get anything so I got me a six pack of beer, a large bottle of Scotch liquor and something to smoke. That's just like the devil. That week I partied and partied. As I was talking to friends, I said, "I'm going to church Sunday."

They laughed at me and said, "You not going to church. Look at you all high up," and I said, "Yes I am."

Sunday came and I went to church, sick, head hurting and my breath smelling like a bar but I went with a hangover and all, and I was glad I did. I didn't get saved that day, but I walked out of Church feeling better than I went in.

God began to deal with me very heavy. I couldn't explain it at that time, but I knew He was talking to me about myself. It's good when God can talk to you and tell you about yourself. I remember one Saturday night a voice spoke to me and told me not to go out, and to tell my friend I wouldn't be going out any more with him. I went anyway. I called myself having a last night outing.

When I sat down in the car, this same voice spoke to me and said, "You having it your way."

I said, "No I'm not having it my way."

So that same voice told me, "You still have to tell him."

I said, "Okay."

That voice spoke again, "Tell him."

I said within myself, *this voice is going to keep on saying the same thing until I give in.* So I told my friend, "This is my last night hanging." He laughed about it and called me crazy because he said never had a woman ever told him that in his life time.

So I said, "This woman just did." and I told him "I want something different in life like going to church."

He said, "There's nothing going on in church but a lot of noise and pretenders claiming something that they are not."

I was uncomfortable just them few minute being in the midst of his presence. He was talking crazy using all kind of foul language. Later on I told him to drop me off in midtown to catch the bus to New York so I went to the City. As I was on the bus, God visited me the whole ride there. He told me what I must do. Yes, I had a conversation with the Lord. I told Him maybe if I move back to New York, things will be better for me.

He let me know that He is everywhere and He said, "I am the same God in New Jersey as in New York." Jesus told me to give my life to Him, and He said, "I have a work for you to do."

I said, "Who me?"

He said, "Yes."

I was puzzled. I just didn't get it. As the days, weeks, and months went by in different parts of the city I would hear preachers on the street preaching. At times someone would witness to me about the Lord and I was just like some people today saying I don't want to hear or I'm not ready. Sometimes I crossed the street to the other side so they wouldn't bother me. To me it seemed like I was trying to blot things out of my mind and knowing that I was tired and ready to make a change.

Jesus let me know about the new birth, and being born again. I took it to heart and went to that church on the highway where Evelyn and Mary went. As soon as I walked in the door, I felt the presence of the Lord. Within myself, I knew, *This is what I wanted. This is one of the parts missing from my life. This is my new beginning,* I started seeking the Lord. I liked the singing, the praying and the people were praising God. Few in number but the Spirit of the Lord was all in that place. All I could do was cry saying, "This is what I want."

In late October of 1975, Jesus saved me. I joined the church, went about three weeks and stopped going to church because the enemy had offered me something that my flesh liked, and that's partying and drinking, and everything was free. When I wasn't doing what the devil told me, I didn't get free things like that, so that's what he offered me so I could stay with him along with other things.

The Pastor called me and asked me how I was doing because she had not seen me. The Pastor told me, "This is your new beginning in Christ Jesus and to keep what you received from Christ, you must stay in church. Pastor also let me know the order of the services. So I started out by coming to noonday prayer. I obeyed the Pastor and followed everywhere the church went. This ministry was so great. They believed in shut-ins, fasting and praying. The Pastor lived the life that she teaches, "Holiness or Hell."

One day, after noonday prayer at church, my Pastor and I went to our mothers of the church's homes to have prayer. They were unable to come to church so we went to them and had prayer. When we had that last prayer, that third prayer it was December 13, 1975. Jesus came into that prayer meeting, right in the mother's kitchen and baptized me with the Holy Ghost. I felt as though I was out of this world, and that was the other part of the missing pieces. I can't really describe it. You have to experience it for yourself. Hallelujah!

CHAPTER 3

DREAMS THAT CAME TRUE

In the year 1976, the first week of October, I had a dream and in this dream I saw a young man and he was put out of this church because of a lifestyle he wanted to keep. God wasn't pleased with it because this young man thought he was okay. He felt like nothing was wrong with being a homosexual and doing a work for the Lord.

One night we had service in downtown Elizabeth in a building the Lord blessed the church with for only a dollar. That was on a Wednesday night, the third week of October. The church doors opened and in walked a young man. My eyes opened very wide and I said within myself *Oh! My God! This is my dream that I dreamed.* I looked at him and he had a homosexual spirit on him, a young man that needed help. At that time I was young in the Lord and there was a lot I didn't understand. In this life, keep on living and you will understand it better by and by.

He started coming to our services often so our Pastor gave him something to do in the church. He said that he is an Evangelist. As days, weeks, and months passed by, we found out that he was a gifted and talented young man. He knew how to set up a church, do fund raisers, play all types of instruments, beat the drums, train people's voices to sing, and also he could preach. He knew the Word of God. When you are gifted like that, there are many things I know for a fact – you must stay humble, seek God's face, fast, pray and be watchful because the enemy will set you up for his service. See the enemy wants to be like God.

After being with us the first six months, my Pastor made him her Assistant Pastor. See all of us – her spiritual children were young in the Lord. She did everything – preach on Sunday morning, teach Bible studies on Tuesday, teach on Friday evening and when we had appointments to go to other churches, she did the preaching. We went into hospitals, and homes to pray for the sick and I was in the class of learning.

Listen, on this journey your body does get tired along the way. To all Pastors you have to hold on and give it to God. He sees and knows that you need help in the ministry. In (Isaiah 40:31 the Bible states: *But they that wait upon the Lord shall renew their strength; they shall mount up with wings as eagles; they shall run, and not be weary; and they shall walk, and not faint.* So wait on the Lord. He shall renew your strength in due time.

What I have learned down through the years and seen how the enemy operates is it's worth suffering and being tired in the body rather than putting an outsider who you don't know over your people that God called you to flock. God will raise up somebody in your house of worship – someone you birthed, who got saved in your ministry, who you fasted for and with, who you stayed at church with until they came through. Those are the ones that you know and when the ripe time comes, God will speak to you and let you know it's time for that person to go forward over the affair.

Doing a work for the Lord, you have to commit yourself to fasting, praying, seeking God and being very watchful. That's one thing the enemy doesn't like for you to do is to be committed unto the Lord. The same enemy that I saw at the beginning is the same enemy right now. He's trying to find a way to destroy the works of God. Yes, we have an enemy who's on the run twenty four hours each and every day. Don't let the enemy run you off the track. Let the Word hit him.

See I was a dreamer. You know when you do a lot of fasting and praying, the gifts from God will operate in your life and my Pastor had us fasting. I would fast when no one else would fast. Gifts will come but they don't stay because that gift might not be for you. God gives to us according to our ability. He knows we can't handle certain gifts or that a certain gift is not for you. Then again God has another gift that He knows you will able to work with. God let us know His word is real. One night I dreamed that I was in the center of a large room, and this same young man took my left hand and my Pastor took my right hand. He was pulling me toward him; he told me to follow him, and my Pastor was pulling me toward her and told me that he will lead me the wrong way. I was halted between two opinions, puzzled and confused in the mind. By me being young in the Lord, I thought this young man was a man of God. Great gifts work without repentance and you can be fooled by them. My Pastor was a woman who prays, fasts and is always seeking the Lord. I'm glad she won me over.

It's something when you dream a lot and don't understand it. This third dream I dreamed about this same young man dressed up in a robe but he had a black cape covering him. He was sitting in a big seat in a high place where it was only him alone. I was scared. I told one of the sisters of the church about this dream of this young man. She told me I shouldn't have said that about him. Me with no understanding, I began to pray and I asked the Lord why is he like this? At that time I didn't get an answer from God.

Then I prayed and asked God to give me an understanding about that dream. Still no answer. People of God, at times there is a waiting period. God doesn't always answer you right away. Keep on living. You will understand it better by and by. This young man was trying to get it together, but it seemed like he didn't want to do what it would take for him to get delivered. He went in great error and attached with souls that love him and some of them are led astray and some backslide, and you know what? The blood is on his hands.

I'm telling you how the enemy operates and how he uses people. As time passed, this young man had a terrible takeover spirit. He stopped preaching what God gave him and started preaching what his followers told him about what was going on in the church. There was no anointing. He was always speaking in tongues calling himself prophesying while tearing up the church, beating the walls and the floor of the church, and acting unseemly. God wasn't in that. That's what happens when you are not seeking the Lord. There's an open door for the devil to come in. The enemy will have you doing unseemly things.

Who-so-ever reads this book, stay on fire for God. I have a question for you. Do you know what time it is? It's time to turn right and go straight, stay prayed up, and fast and stay into the Word of God. Above all, be watchful. Our enemy, the devil is on his job twenty-four seven. He's not playing. But he has his plan laid out to try to get you and me in his trap. Don't let him get you; we have a lot of the Word of God to put on him.

It took a preacher from another church that rendered us a service, in fact that was a service for the young man. Anyway, this Pastor told my Pastor not to let this young man tear up her church. This young man got mad and told my Pastor, "Why you let a preacher from another church come in to tell you how to run your church?"

There were many Christians that came to our noonday prayer and some people in the neighborhood also were coming. All of a sudden, they stopped coming.

Many of the Christians were praying for us. Bad news travels more than good news. We lost our building downtown that the Lord blessed us with. It seemed like a curse fell on the church. We almost got put out of our church uptown. We couldn't pay rent because the young man was spending our church money. It's something being put out your place of worship because of not paying rent, and we are serving a God that blesses and makes a way for His people. In the midst of that problem, God stepped in and fixed it for us. Thank You Jesus.

The enemy used that young man; he didn't care about the church or its members, and he had no respect for the Pastor. He was turned over to the enemy. He didn't work; he didn't have a job. Another two months passed where he saved our church money so he prepared himself a wedding. He got married in another church to a young girl round about his age. That spirit of the devil came out in him full force. It was one of those cover ups.

He said, "So what I'm marrying her? It's not going stop me from sleeping with men." How low the enemy can carry you with no shame. That marriage didn't last long.

What I'm writing is true. Many times when he got sick, My Pastor and I would go to his house to see him. He'd be in bed very weak, body messed up, blood all over the place – in the bed, all on the sheets. All he could do was lay there in pain in his back bottom. Within myself I was praying. I asked the Lord to touch him. I looked at him and he looked very confused in the mind and foolish in the face. He didn't want to be like that but the enemy had him and gave him a spirit of pride. He kept saying, "I will be okay."

My Pastor said, "Are you sure you're okay?" and he said, "I'm okay."

You can't play with the devil. He will put sport on you.

CHAPTER 4

WHAT'S HAPPENING NOW?

This is my experience that I'm sharing with you. Today, there are many free agents, some are church hoppers. Some come in sheep's clothing, but they are wolves. Some are just plain undercover – people that the enemy uses trying to destroy God's work. These types of people, he makes them sometime take their own lives when he has no more use for them. It's sad when you stop seeking God.

Finally, the Lord delivered us from that problem. This young man left our church. The last I heard about this young man, he was in a shelter and that is very sad. He had no mind to live for the Lord. The enemy has no more use for him. He's just sitting back laughing at him, most likely calling him a fool. That's how the enemy operates. He strips you of everything that you once had in Christ Jesus, then he goes to the next person to see how he can get that one. Make sure you're not the next victim in line. The enemy is full of drama, I see where people go to the building which they call church and can tell you about how good their Pastor preached, and tell you what the message was all about. Right after that, the devil uses them with much fowl language or bad words coming from their mouth, and the first thing they say is "Excuse me. That slipped."

Oh no, that didn't slip. It was there all the time. They have never been clean on the inside. The devil has them telling other people how to live right or you should not do this or that, and at times they tell you that what you're doing is wrong and they haven't been saved themselves. These people belong to the building not the church, because the Church is a body of baptized believers who are saved on the day of Pentecost until the rapture of the church. These building people need you and me to witness to them and tell them about Jesus Christ so they won't be lost. Once they get saved they too can be the Church. There are those who're claiming salvation and have left God. In other words, they divorced God; and by them divorcing God, they are committing adultery. Yes I'm talking about spiritual adultery. Now the enemy has them sleeping with him. Many say they are not doing that. I'm serving you notice that yes, you are. By you sleeping with the enemy, he will have you doing what the world does – picking up the characteristics of the world by being their friend and doing what they are doing – unrighteous acts. You can't be on God's side and the world's.

Satan desires to seduce us into his set-up system which is submitting to his authority. All he wants us to do is bow and worship him but the Word says in James 4:7 *Submit yourselves therefore to God. Resist the devil, and he will flee from you.* The more we seek God, the closer we draw to Him and He draws closer to us, and as we stay humble in the Lord, in due time He shall lift us up. In life itself there is a lot of temptation out there but as long as we do what the Word says do, we are on safe ground and we have victory in Christ Jesus. Do you believe it? Well I do.

In September 1978, God called me into the ministry. The enemy fought me so hard that I didn't want to pick up my calling in Christ Jesus. I lost my memory for about two or three weeks, I remember one day in noonday prayer, I was praising God and my praises turned into, "Yes Lord I will go where you want me to go, and I will say what you want me to say." The Lord didn't let me rest until I became obedient to His will.

I was raised in a church where they told us that a woman is not permitted to speak in the church, should remain silent and ask her husband when she gets home. They interpreted the Word of God the wrong way or they had no understanding of that Scripture *(1 Corinthians 14:34-35).* The enemy will blind your eyes and will have you twisting the Word of God around or have you taking away from or adding to the Word. My Bible says in (Revelation 22:18b-19) *If any man shall add unto these things, God shall add unto him the plagues that are written in this book. And if any man shall take away from the words of the book of this prophecy, God shall take away his part out of the book of life, and out of the holy city, and from the things which are written in this book.* People are sleeping and letting the enemy fool them into tampering with the Word of God. This is a careful walk with the Lord. A small thing will stop us from making it to the Kingdom of heaven. Please don't let the enemy blindfold your eyes because if he does, you're going to fall just like him. See, you can get back up and ask for forgivingness; he can't. He once had a chance but he blew it. That's why he's working so hard to have many with him in Hell being tormented.

In the year 1978 I made my announcement that the Lord called me to preach His Word. When you make up your mind and say yes to the Lord, the enemy will manifest himself full force. He did in my case. He knew that he had lost me. Yes, I changed bosses. When I was with the enemy, he gave me his title to assist him with his bad work. I was on a mission for the devil and was on dangerous ground. I didn't know I was on my way to Hell. But God rescued me. Thank God for the blood of Jesus. Day by day, your walk with the Lord will cost you. It's worth it all. I'm glad I am on the Lord's side.

CHAPTER 5

ADJUSTMENTS

I had to make some adjustments in my life. Number one was to stay in the church. Number two was to have a prayer life. Number three to fast, and number four to be watchful on every side. It takes all of that and more. You must stay busy for the Lord, read the Word of God and eat the Word of God. Don't think you have it made because everything is going smooth. It just takes a second for you to be off guard and the enemy will zero in on you. He's laying there in wait for the moment to catch us off guard. Anytime you keep letting the enemy trick you with the same thing over and over again, you are off guard. If you haven't started, try now to make some adjustments.

Carnal weapons don't count when you are fighting the enemy. Paul tells us in (2 Corinthians 10:4) *For the weapons of our warfare are not carnal, but mighty through God to the pulling down of strong holds;* We have to realize we are in a spiritual battle. If we don't use the weapons God provides for us, we will lose lots of battles in this life. If your weapons are carnal that's the tool the enemy uses, and he will use you to carry out his so called plan.

God wants us to stand up for what's right. Paul says in (2 Corinthians 10:5) *Casting down imaginations, and every high thing that exalteth itself against the knowledge of God and bringing into captivity every thought to the obedience of Christ.* It's time to cast down every imagination that the enemy has worked up in the mind – even the high place where he has fooled you having you thinking that it's alright. See the enemy has exalted himself against the knowledge of God and he's trying to place that spirit on us. We can say, "Devil you are a liar and the father of lies In the name of Jesus."

We are accused of many different things. In the Bible many were accused also, but they came out victorious. We can too if we stand up for what is right. As we walk by faith, we are wearing righteousness. That is the "armor" Paul is speaking of in Ephesians 6:13.

There's a question Paul has for us and we can always say as it says in (Romans 8:35, 37) *"Who can separate us the love of Christ? Shall tribulation, or distress, or persecution, or famine, or nakedness, or peril, or sword..........Nay in all these (strongholds) things, we are more than conquerors through him that loved us."* We will have trials, but our trials won't defeat us. We have to remember who's on our side. God has given us His Word to stand on and to protect our thoughts and emotions'

One of the greatest weapons the enemy tries is false accusations. They can come from other people or from within ourselves. We need to remember that our enemy instigated them. You need to continue to put on the breastplate of God's righteousness. Just remember we are wearing the righteousness in our heart. This makes us the accepted in His beloved. Paul says in Ephesians 1:6 *"To the praise of the glory of his grace, wherein he hath made us accepted in the beloved."* There are so many great promises in the Word of God. Who wouldn't serve a great God who loves His people? Think! Only God can give you what you need and a great calmness of peace. I know. I didn't have peace. I had no joy. I wasn't happy. I was always sad. Then along came Jesus and mended all my broken pieces. What He did for me, He can do for you. There is no secret what God can do. If He's done it for others, He will do it for you and nothing is too hard for the Lord. He can do anything.

How far the enemy can take you. Before you know it, he has you. When I think about that, my mind goes back into the book of Genesis at the beginning of the third chapter, where it says that the serpent was more subtil. This creature which is less than a man – the enemy comes in any form, fashion, beauty – it doesn't matter to him but when he comes, he's there to take you and before you know it, he has you and all it takes is just a conversation. But why will you hold a conversation with the enemy? He's very sneaky and tries to make things seem very real to you. That's what happened to Eve. Her mistake was holding a conversation with him. In the Bible (2 Corinthians 11:14) states: *And no marvel; for Satan himself is transformed into an angel of light.*

In the Scriptures, the serpent Satan appeared as an angel of light. In Revelation 12:9 it states: *And the great dragon was cast out that old serpent called the Devil and Satan which deceiveth the whole world: he was cast out into the earth, and his angels were cast out with him.* There is no room in God's kingdom for wrong doing. There is no room for anything but the righteousness of God. There is no sin in heaven, so don't even think that you can do what you want to do in this life and go to heaven. We've got to repent and ask Jesus to come into our life and save us. None but the righteous shall see God.

CHAPTER 6

STAND AND STAY STABLE

When we take a stand on the gospel, God gives us exactly what we need to defeat the enemy and to hold our ground. He will give us stability. There are many Christians today who are not taking a stand. They are unstable and have been tossed to and fro. They are carried about with every wind and doctrine. The devil gives them just what they want to hear when they are going through and what the devil does is twist The Word of God to fit them and unaware, they accept it because it sounds good to their ears.

Unstable Christians aren't grounded in the Word of God. When you are unstable, that's an easy entrance open for the enemy to come in easily and lead you astray. We must stay in the Word of God, and apply it to our lives. You will then know when the enemy comes. Remember he comes with lies, and he loves to change things. Get the picture. Our conflict is not with our sisters or brothers. It's with the enemy who uses people. Some people deny the existence of demonic powers. We who believe the Word of God know these powers exist. With the help of his demonic forces out looking to see what vessel of God is open for them to enter into so they can use them, Satan himself can accomplish his will by sending out all different ranks of demons. The sad part about this is he uses people to do his evil work.

Satan has his forces of evil well organized. He has a great conspiracy going on the power of his authority. He is the ruler of the darkness of this world and spiritual wickedness, plotting to do us in. God's got his number. It won't be long. Jesus is coming. So I'm telling all saved people to hold on. Don't give up. Don't give in to the enemy's tricks. Go through since Jesus died on the cross for you and me. We have that assurance of peace with God in the midst of it all. Listen. If you're not completely prepared and protected, the enemy will destroy you. So make sure you're dwelling in the secret place of the Most High and if you are, you shall abide under the shadow of the Almighty. God will protect you from the enemy's darts. He throws some very hard and sharp darts at you and knocks you off guard. He stays ready to target anybody he can – the young ones as well as the old.

Everything we need is in the Word of God. Our God designed His Word for our protection from the enemy. We shouldn't try to look in two directions at the same time. We can't look to God and want to look in the world at the same time. The world will fail you but there is no failure in God. What I mean is if you are living for God then you can't live like the world. The Word of God says in (Matthew 6:24) *No man can serve two masters: for either he will hate the one, and love the other; or else he will hold to the one, and despise the other. Ye cannot serve God and mammon.*

We are serving a Holy God; He brought us out of the bondage of sin, and we shouldn't have another god before Him. God said in His Word that He is a jealous God. Yet and still He shows mercy unto them that He loves. God loves us. That's why He sent His Son to die for us. He wants us to serve Him in truth. The enemy messed up so bad, the Lord prescribed a remedy to solve the problem. If He didn't, we would all be lost, and I thank God for sending His Son, and I thank His Son for being obedient to the Father. Can't nobody tell me that God isn't real and that He doesn't love us.

All those unbelievers that the enemy has fooled, telling them there is no God, your day is coming where you're going to take your bow and confess that Jesus Christ is Lord. It's in the Word of God, (Philippians 2:10-11) states: *That at the name of Jesus every knee should bow, of things in heaven, and things in the earth, and things under the earth; and that every tongue should confess that Jesus Christ is Lord, to the glory of God the Father.* The Word of God is true and He said in His Word let every man be a liar. Many people today don't believe in God's Word and that's because they don't read The Word of God.

CHAPTER 7

HOLD ON TO GOD

In your Christian walk, have you ever experienced when going forward in Christ, somehow there was a setback? It feels as though you aren't getting anywhere. It means you have entertained the enemy along the way. Come on and confess that once upon a time the enemy had a hold on your mind, and the enemy still has a hold on some people's minds. We all have experienced that, including me. I prayed for a lot of things at that time believing God, and somehow I was getting nowhere. A spirit of doubt ran through my mind.

Yours might not be doubt, it could be something else. Like fear. Sometimes we think it's an emotion, but we need to realize that it's a spirit and that's what the enemy will throw on us and if we're not watchful, we will receive it from him. He loves to torment people because he is tormented himself. Every so often he loves to speak to you and make you think that God doesn't love you. He will ask you why you believe in a God that's not real. The devil will go on to tell you that there is no hope in that God that you are serving. That makes a lot of sense to him – intimidate us with fear. He is doing all he can to pull us with him. Pull your mind in, go forward, and stay focused on the Lord and stay in the "Word of God." You can't go wrong by staying in the Word of God.

The enemy discourages us, trying to make us feel like we are nothing. He wants you to have a pity party so you can look down on yourself and dwell on those seeds he has sown in your mind. If you entertain it, it will go to your heart than the enemy will have you walking around saying, *I'm not going to be nothing in life* and he will add that you're going to be a failure. He tries to frustrate us until we are ready to quit. That's his job to do that. Don't quit! Hold on to God. I'm telling you again the enemy's time is almost up. When you feel discouraged and hopeless, speak to that problem and as you speak to that problem, believe and hold on to God. Don't let Him go. Many Christians today let go because they didn't have that strong and solid grip on the Lord like they should have. They didn't seek Him constantly. Sometimes we are a once-in-a-while seeker and that's no good. In (Amos 5:4) it states: *For thus saith the Lord unto the house of Israel, Seek ye me, and ye shall live.* God told the house of Israel to seek Him. The same Word of God is for us today. God is looking for continual and constant seekers. That's the only way you and I are going to survive in this life. We must seek the Lord while He may be found and call upon Him while He is near: all those wicked ways that the devil gave to us, we have to forsake them and all our unrighteous thoughts that are not of God. The Word (Isaiah 55:8) states: *For my thoughts are not your thoughts, neither are your ways my ways, saith the LORD.*

Instability is a serious problem which can hinder or destroy your walk with God. Stay stable in Christ Jesus. The Bible contains warnings also about being unstable. In the Bible (James 1:8) states *"A double-minded man is unstable in all his ways."* In order to remain stable you can't be double-minded. Whatever you are asking God for, believe Him and it shall come to pass. Many saints who once believed God have taken a back seat and given birth to doubt because instability set in their minds then into the heart, and that's how it gave birth. You know the enemy will add, along with doubt, temptation; and if you get drawn away in that direction of lust, when lust conceives it brings forth sin, and sin when it's finished with you it brings forth death. What can you do when you are spiritually or naturally dead? The answer is nothing. If we don't give our lives to the Lord, we're going to miss out and go to a Christ-less grave.

CHAPTER 8

WHEN DOUBT SETS IN

There are some problems the enemy will frequently throw at you. He'll try sickness, financial loss, and broken family relationships, among others. He may try to hit you with emotional darts of anger, fear, depression, self pity and along with all that, doubt. Get strong in the Lord by fasting, praying, reading and eating the Word of God and doing what the Word tells you to do. If you don't, you will not make it. You will die a spiritual death.

The enemy doesn't give up or in. He will cause confusion among the saints. The Bible, in (1 Corinthians 14:33) says *For God is not the author of confusion, but of peace a*s *in all churches of the saints.* I'm not speaking of a church "building."

We are the church – a body of baptized believers who are saved for the day of Pentecost until the day of the rapture. We need to resist the enemy's efforts in confusing us, by relying on the strength of the Lord.

Sometimes in life the mind can get afflicted because of a bad case of doubt that has set in. Don't let the enemy take you down like that. He will rock you to sleep. In (1 Thessalonians 5:6) it states, *Therefore let us not sleep, as do other; but let us watch and be sober.* We are children of the light and of the day. Don't let darkness overtake you as a thief. Watch "yourself" so you won't be overtaken by the enemy.

After the first two years of my calling in the Lord, the enemy showed up big time. Things got rough. I remember our Pastor called for a church shut-in. She said, "Put your family and loved ones names in the prayer box at the altar." We went five days and five nights fasting and praying every three hours around the clock. As time went by my mother, sisters, and brothers got saved. The enemy got mad because my family was taken out of his hands. Since then he has been on my trail. When the Lord saves you, reach back for your family. I did. God is concerned about you and your household – family first then it spreads abroad. Jesus doesn't want us to be lost. He loves us. He paid the price for us on Calvary. Now it's time to go out into the vineyard and win souls. In (Matthew 9:37-38) it states: *Then saith he unto his disciples, The harvest truly is plenteous, but the laborers are few; Pray ye therefore the Lord of the harvest, that he will send forth laborers into his harvest.* There's a lot of work that needs to be done out in the field. God is looking for laborers to put in the field. So many laborers when they first gave their life to the Lord and were called into the ministries where they work, God blessed them and then they quit. Some got lazy on the job and some the enemy fooled. In case you didn't know this, it is a life-time job until Jesus comes. See, God will pay you for what you do. The enemy has many working for him right in the church – no souls are being saved just a gathering putting on their program. The Spirit of God is no where around. They have put Jesus on the outside because they don't have no room for Him.

CHAPTER 9

DIDN'T WORK

I remember traveling to North Carolina with the flyers to pass out to every home down in that area as we were paying the tolls to get off of New Jersey turnpike on to I-95, the enemy jumped in my car and it cut off. I was on a mission to deliver the flyers in North Carolina and as we were sitting in my car with no power, we didn't know what was wrong.

There was a car behind us. This man asked me what was wrong. I told him that I didn't know, so he asked, "Where are you all going?" I told him we were on a mission for the Lord and about the service we were having in North Carolina and that we were on our way down so we can pass out the flyers to the people so they will know about the service. He told us he was going to some part of Virginia, but they were willing to give us a ride. So I asked him if he don't mind could he push my car to the gas station and give us a ride to Washington, DC, where my niece was and she would take us the rest of the way. He asked, "What about your car?" I told him, "I will take care of the car when I come back though this way." What the man did, let us have the front seat. He let me drive his car to Washington, DC. I offered to pay the driver of the car or give him gas money, and he said, "No, but you could pray for us."

The enemy will try to see what you're going to do when trouble comes and at the same time, God has a ram in the bush. The enemy tried all he could, but it didn't work.

I loved being out in the field setting up crusades, preparing for my Pastor to preach. We went into homes, passed out flyers for the event and we witnessed. The Lord blessed each evening of the crusades. Deliverance was in the house, souls got saved, the sick got healed and many that were bound were set free by the Word of God.

I learned a lot from the Woman of God, and as the years passed, she appointed me to be her assistant in the church. For fifteen years I was her assistant, obeying what she instructed me to do while she was in the field.

I thank God for the experience I gained during those years. It wasn't easy. I encountered disappointments, being mistreated, among other things I was talked about, I was hurt, and many of times I felt like giving up. I prayed and told God about it. He let me know I was being made for the work He has for me to do. I thanked God in the midst of it all. The enemy is a liar. I gained the most – more love, knowledge and understanding in how to treat people. I'm holding on to all the good and righteous things Christ has for me.

By the way, when I came back to take care of my car, it wasn't a big problem. God will put people in your way to help you out. My car got fixed and I was on my way back to New Jersey. The enemy wanted us to turn around and go back home. He didn't want us to pass those flyers out. And when the service started in North Carolina, The Lord saved, blessed, healed and souls got delivered.

Nobody's mad but the devil. The next night the one that opened the doors for service was late, we waited and prayers were made without ceasing. Then the man came and opened the doors. He seemed like he didn't want to be there. I know when things happen like that the blessing of the Lord is in the house. The enemy tried to stop the service many of times and many ways, but he couldn't because God's in control. We who are in Christ Jesus must realize that God is in control. Our life is in His hands and can't no devil in Hell have the say so. Yes, he can come and stir up stuff.

Think! How far can he go? As long as we are in Christ Jesus and His Word is abiding on the inside of us, the Word will make the enemy tremble. He knows there is a God. He knows

about God and he got to know God better when
he tried to take over. It didn't work.

CHAPTER 10

IN THIS WORLD TROUBLE

In this world, we will have trouble. Jesus said in (John 16:33) *These things I have spoken unto you, that in me ye might have peace. In the world ye shall have tribulation: but be of good cheer, I have overcome the world.* When you are on a mission for Jesus, you will encounter trouble from both the outside and the inside. What I am saying is you will encounter trouble from the enemy, the world, and your own flesh that will resist and pressure you to do wrong.

The devil will speak and want you to do what he tells you to do. He doesn't want you to do God's will. It's our decision whether or not to exercise the authority Jesus obtained over the enemy. The enemy is like a UPS delivery man or the mailman. We have authority from the Lord. Jesus' authority doesn't do us any good unless we appreciate it.

See when the enemy comes knocking at your door and if you give in to him, that's a chance for him to deliver whatever package he has for you. And if you're so far gone by not being watchful, right then and there you're receiving what he has to offer. God gave us the power and authority. So I am telling you to exercise what you have and if you do nothing, you receive nothing. The authority we assert over the enemy depends upon the victory Jesus won over Satan. You and I can't defeat the devil on our own, it's Christ in us. Make sure you have Christ anchored in you. He is that solid rock.

The enemy doesn't want us to go the right way. He makes us feel the right way is too hard. The Word of God says in (Proverbs 13:15) *Good understanding giveth favor: but the way of transgressors is hard.* As long as we live in this troubled world, Jesus Christ is the best thing that could happen to us. We were lost once upon a time and now Jesus found us. If everybody gets Jesus in their life, they will gain salvation and He will see you through.

One of the things we must do is submit ourselves to the Lord. By learning and obeying His Word. We will then have God's power and authority to resist the devil. In (James 4:7) it states: *Submit yourselves therefore to God. Resist the devil and he will flee from you.* Our "enemy" will take flight (he will flee....) but we have to submit ourselves to God. (James 4:8b) states, *Draw nigh to God, and he will draw nigh to you.* Put the Word on the enemy, which is the sword of the Spirit. Learn how to use it, Jesus did. And you can learn how to use the Word if you stay in the Word of God and apply to your life on a daily basis.

CHAPTER 11

GET TO KNOW GOD

We really need to seek a true relationship with God. There is something in us that makes us afraid of the commitment connected to the true intimacy with God. For one thing, it requires purity. It's time out for dating God. In other words, we act like a man or woman with no love there. She's going with him to get what she wants and he's going with her to get what he wants. Every time he or she needs they go and get. That's what you call using a person. That's the same way we do God, use Him. We need to be sincere, and stop using Him, that's worldly material of the enemy. Put on the ring of commitment, and live for God. Get to know God, and stop letting the enemy control you.

God is looking for real people who are willing to live for Him. He wants us to go out into the highways and vineyards and work. But first let the Lord work in you then you'll be ready to work out in the vineyard. There's plenty of work to do. Let me remind you again that the enemy has his numbers out in the field working for him. We are God's ambassadors and we are making a poor candidate for doing The Lord's will. We are letting the enemy have the right away in our lives.

I want to be the one in the field, where no one wants to go. I'm not satisfied in just preaching in the churches. Right now, it's time to get out into the street, hospitals, jail houses, nursing homes, family homes and tell the people that are saved to get in a hurry and that He's coming back for people who are ready to go back with Him. My daily prayer is for the Lord to steer me in the right direction, where I'm needed. Getting to know God more and more and loving souls, I have a mind and desire to do all that I can to win souls to Christ.

When you get to know God, you will hunger and thirst after righteousness. He will satisfy your soul. We are so busy asking God for things that satisfy not. God sees and knows our needs. He said in (Philippians 4:19) *But my God shall supply all your need according to his riches and glory by Christ Jesus.*

We like to say "Lord I want" but God said I will supply all your needs. In (Psalms 37-4) it states: *Delight thyself also in the Lord; and he shall give thee the desires of thine heart.* Seek God and repent. Let Him move on the altar of your heart that the cleansing fire may fall upon you. God is concerned about the whole man, as

60

it is referenced in (3 John 2) *Beloved I wish above all things that thou mayst prosper and be in health, even as thy soul prospereth.* The enemy wants us to prosper in him and not in God. When you do that you are headed the wrong way. God wants us to prosper. He's concerned about the whole man. He loves us.

God continuously tells us in the Bible that He has our future in His hand. The enemy's time is almost out. God promises to lead us. The Bible tells us how He has proven Himself faithful to others as He led them, In (Proverbs 3:5) it states: *Trust in the Lord with all thine heart; and lean not unto thine own understanding.* God wants us to grow, believe, and trust in Him at all times. Don't even lean on your own understanding.

If we lean on our own understanding, we are headed on a downward road to destruction. In (Proverbs 3:6) it states: *In all thy ways acknowledge him, and he shall direct thy paths.* God is trustworthy. He wants you to get everything you need for this journey. God knows all about the enemy and the things he tries to pull. There's work to be done out there and a question to us like in the book of (Isaiah 6:8b) states: *Whom shall I send, and who shall go for us? Then Isaiah answered, "Here am I send me."* God is looking for another Isaiah who's ready to sell out for the Lord and go in the vineyard and work. There are many Christians who want to go but they still have their grave clothes on. I know that you are reading this book and saying what do she mean when she say grave clothes on? Well many today say they are Christian, but haven't repented and asked the Lord to come into their life and save them, and after that they need the Holy Spirit in their lives. Not only that but they have to study and eat the Word of God.

Having the proper clothing on reminds you that this is a spiritual warfare and you have to have what it takes in dealing with our enemy to work in the field. You have to know what you're doing because the enemy is out there. You won't last a second if you're not equipped with the Word of God and have not experienced anything. One thing about this book is that it mostly tells how you must have the Word of God because that's what it takes to fight the enemy. What do you think?

Do you have something else to fight the devil with? Did I miss something unaware? I don't think so. The Word will give us victory; so let this book bless your heart and push you to start seeking God in the fullness.

The Bible is full of scripture verses reminding the people of the things God has done for them. In order to move forward in the Lord, you must stay in the Word of God, and don't let the enemy get the victory. When he comes, put the Word on him. The devil is watching his clock and he knows time is running out for him. Just to let you know it won't be long. So don't throw away your confidence; it will be richly rewarded. You need to persevere and when you have done the will of God, you will receive His promises.

The Holy Spirit can give us victory, since the Spirit's power is imparted through prayer and fasting. Not only does the Holy Spirit empower us for battle, but He also enables us to pray in the Lord's will. Our prayers should be sincere and heartfelt. As you pray, it's important that you remain alert. Pray with your eyes always on the enemy, lest he moves in and defeats you with his deceptive tactics. Watch. Watch, and I say unto you, watch while you pray.

You have to understand that you are a child of the King. We are saved. We are no longer children tossed to and fro, carried about with every wind of doctrine, by the sleight of men's cunning craftiness whereby they lie in wait to deceive you (one of the enemy's tricks). You can't believe everything you hear and see. The good part about this is our life is hidden with Christ. Yes, the enemy comes with his deceiving spirit, his craftiness, and all kinds of tricks. You're going to be hated for the sake of Christ; you must remember the one that endureth to the end shall be saved.

As I read the Word of God, Paul stressed the importance of growing up and maturing as Christians. In my lifetime, I became as a little small child-like Christian. At one time, I believed anything and anyone. I was a baby in the Lord. I lacked the experience and education to exercise discernment. The Bible says you will know them by their fruit. The words they say seem real to you, until you're constantly around them. That's why you need to study the "Word of God." Put God's Words in you, and you will grow in the Lord. You're going to come up against a lot of the enemy's tricks.

It's sad to get trapped in the arms of Satan sitting right in the church, and him having you feeling there's no way out. The devil doesn't care how much you go to church. He doesn't care how much you fast. Speaking of fasting, I remember when we were in church on a 72 hour fast, and the devil through a person came to the church to take me out. He doesn't care how much you pray. He doesn't care how much you help in the ministries, and he doesn't care how much you read or study the "Word of God." The enemy is bold with his evil spirits. He is not ashamed of his game. If you're not watchful, he will zero in on you and use you as one of his tools. Never, never think you have it made because you are saved. That's when the fight begins. Don't even think you have everything under control. That's the lie he told. The enemy is a tamperer; he will mess with you to see what makes you tick. He starts with your faith in God and tries to work where it hurts the most in your life. Sometimes we think that we have conquered a certain area in our life, and don't need God's protection anymore. That is when the devil will attack us. I'm telling you to correct that problem, we need God at all times.

People today haven't corrected that problem that they let the enemy create. Some of them have been in the Lord over ten years or more. Church people walking around with the enemy having them feeling "I'm okay" but they are not. They are messed up. They have no conscience walking around trying to do a work for the Lord. My Bible in (Matthew 7:22) states: *Many will say to me in that day, Lord, Lord have we not prophesied in thy name? and in thy name have cast out devils? and in thy name done many wonderful works? So the Lord answered them* (Matthew 7:23) states: *And then will I profess unto them, I never knew you: depart from me, ye that work iniquity.* '

The Lord lets us know in His Word that not everyone that saith unto Him Lord, Lord shall enter into the Kingdom of heaven. God is looking for "HOLY" people and the enemy knows that. Many today want to work for the Lord but are not willing to sell out and live holy. The devil got them that way. They are in the church just as comfortable as can be. Every so often they do their little body exercise. In (1Timothy 4:8) it states: *For bodily exercise profiteth little: but godliness is profitable unto all things, having promise of the life that now is, and of that which is to come.* At times, they use their gifts. In (Romans 11:29) it states: *For the gifts and calling of God are without repentance.* To all that have gifts, make sure you have Christ in your life. The enemy sees your gifts and he will tell you that you don't need Christ in your life. God wants the gifts to operate in the Churches and it's alright to let your gifts operate in the church, but you have to be living the Word of God. There're going to be a lot of people in Hell with gifts. The enemy has them in a place with him and he's making them feel like it's okay, like you don't have to live Holy or you don't have to seek God. You've been fooled by the enemy. Again, God is looking for HOLY people.

We must realize our conflict is not with people, but with the enemy who uses people. Some deny the existence of demonic powers. We who believe the Word of God know these powers exist. Since the enemy is not omniscient or omnipresent like God, he doesn't know everything. He cannot be everywhere at once. This is why he has a large army of demonic forces. This is how he can operate in many places at one time. With the help of demonic powers, satan himself can accomplish his will. He sends out all different ranks of demons. satan has his force of evil organized greatly. He has a great conspiracy going on the power of his authority. He is the ruler of the darkness of this

GET TO KNOW GOD

world, and spiritual wickedness of plotting to do us in. He robs us of our joy in the Lord. He knows that the joy of the Lord is our strength. He wants to rob us out of our peace. Since Jesus died on the cross, we have peace with God. If we aren't completely prepared and protected, the enemy will destroy us.

As I said before, the enemy discourages us, to make us feel like we are nothing. He wants us to feel like we'll never amount to anything. He tries to frustrate us until we are ready to give up or in to him. Don't give up and don't give in to the devil. Hold on to God's unchanging hand. We must remember the enemy's time is almost up. When you feel discouraged and helpless, speak to that problem. In (1 John 5:4) the Bible states. *For whatsoever is born of God overcometh the world: and this is the victory that overcometh the world even our faith.*

We can say, "Problem, I'm following God's prescribed order." If you believe the Word of God like you should, you can say along with me, "I will overcome the world. I have faith in Christ, and there is therefore now no condemnation in me because I am in Christ Jesus. I am walking in the spirit, not after the flesh. As long as you know you are walking in the spirit of God you are not fulfilling the lust of the flesh. If we are in the flesh, we cannot please God, because the flesh minds the things of the flesh and to be carnally minded is death. The Word of God said to be spiritually minded is life and peace. That's what the enemy doesn't want us to have "LIFE" and "PEACE." He wants us to be just like him – miserable. Keep on living and get God's Word in you like you should. You can't go wrong.

CHAPTER 12

KEEP SELF IN CHECK

The enemy is using lots of evil forces against us. That's why we need to keep self in check. Be careful of what you say, think and do. At times you could be right, and other people could be wrong. Don't make a big show out of it. They might not be where you are in Christ Jesus. If you see that you are indeed right, just pray that God will let them grow in Him. We're all in this together, striving to make it to the city of God.

If you are feeling low in the spirit, go to the throne of grace and pray. You'll feel renewed. In (1 Thessalonians 5:17) it states, *Pray without ceasing.* We have to always pray so we can have strength. We should make our requests known to God, but we should also spend time in prayer and thanksgiving, always making supplication for others. We gain strength by praying, fasting, and reading the Word of God.

Matthew 26:41, states: *Watch and pray, that ye enter not into temptation: the spirit indeed is willing, but the flesh is weak.* The devil, which is our enemy is prowling about like a roaring lion, waiting for a chance to make us slip up. He wants to devour us; "watch your steps" keep self in check at all times so you won't fall. Many Christians today have left God by not keeping self in check. They let the enemy roar in their face and plant a spirit of fear in them. Lots and lots of souls out there are unable to come back to the Lord because of fear.

The enemy has many nasty ways about him. He will catch you off guard by putting you to sleep. He will set-up an activity in your thinking and make you carry out the orders which he prescribed for you. And if you don't keep self in check he will put you on the medication by prescribing a prescription for you. He doesn't care. Whatever he prescribes it will strip off all your blessings from the Lord. He will have your family against you, people in the church against you, plus everyone else against you. Come to yourself and don't wait until it's too late. Don't play with the enemy like Samson did. He played in his weakness (he loved women) but when he came to himself , he realized he lost what he had from God, his strength, his sight, and his freedom. One thing about Samson is that he prayed for God to restore him. See Samson was dedicated by his parents to be a lifelong Nazarite, a person devoted to the Lord's service. Part of that vow included letting his hair grow and abstaining from wine and strong drink.

Samson's strength didn't come from his long hair. His strength came through the Spirit of the "LORD." God restored Samson, but he lost his life.

Don't get caught in a problem like that, seek God and stay in self check. We must correct the wrong things in our life with the Word of God. There are many people around us watching the way we are living. If there is a slip up in our lives, it will be the talk of the town and bad news spreads faster than good news. Don't you want good news to spread around that Jesus Christ is Lord of your life? Bad news is what the enemy likes. That's his game. Listen at this. He's getting into family's homes, disturbing marriages, people's careers and health. One thing for sure, if you are a child of God he will try to stop your progress in living for the Lord. Don't let that be fulfilled in your life, and don't let him stop you from getting to God or living for God; you stop him from not letting you get to God. Enough is enough. We serve a good God that loves His people.

Whenever we are continually disobedient to what God has clearly revealed to us in His Word, we bring ourselves under the influence of a witchcraft curse. I know you are asking "Why?" The reason for this is rebellion, and that's witchcraft. What did the man of God tell King Saul after he disobeyed God? In (1 Samuel 15:23) the Bible states: *For rebellion is as the sin of witchcraft, and stubbornness is as iniquity and idolatry.* King Saul rejected the Word of the Lord. He refused to obey the Word of the Lord. So God rejected him. That's the same spirit our enemy carries around – rebellion against God; and that same spirit is what he is sowing out into the hearts of men today.

I have been in contact with many Christians today who, for whatever reason, live in an almost constant state of disobedience. Watch it!! That's the seed from the enemy. They escape one snare, only to find themselves trapped in another one. Most church goers like to do things their way. I'm not talking about those who are "saved" those who saved are going to live according to the Word of God. Church goers are like the Word says In (Proverbs 14:12) *There is a way which seemeth right unto man, but the end thereof are the ways of death.* When you are headed that way, the enemy is in front of you on death row.

In (Romans 6:23) it states: *For the wages of sin is death; but the gift of God is eternal life through Jesus Christ our lord.* The enemy's deeds are evil. There is no good in him.

CHAPTER 13

CHURCHES WAKE UP

It's time for the Churches to open their eyes, before the sunset. You can escape the devil's traps. In order to do so "WAKE-UP". The enemy is blaming, deceiving and lying to make you feel as though it's alright. He's doing what he's supposed to do. We are not doing what God wants us to do. God's Word exposes deception and discerns the thoughts and the intentions of man's heart. When we are afflicted because we want to do things our way, the devil makes us refuse to learn. He'll have you blaming everyone else instead of learning from the error of your ways and getting up and asking God for forgiveness. Again I say "WAKE UP CHURCHES! STOP! JESUS IS COMING."

Look around. The forces of evil have increased mightily. The enemy has increased with his powerful weapon. It's time for us to pray with all perseverance and supplication so we don't fall. So pull out your weapons of prayer and fasting. Let people know that Jesus is on

His way back to get those who have repented and believed in Him as their personal savior. Eternal life is for everyone who receives God's Son, Jesus, who died and rose from the grave. Living for Christ will last forever. Let Christ rule in your life. You'll see the difference. You'll feel better, walk and talk better. Above all, you'll act better.

Many saints today who have been in the Lord for years and years have cooled off. The old man came back to life. I'm asking all people of God to inventory themselves out and see what they let back into their life. I talk to different people and one of the biggest problems is an attitude problem. They just don't know how to talk to people.

The next problem is a bossy spirit; they like to boss people around. Another problem is a lust spirit. These are some, but there are many more that God's people are letting the enemy use to take full control of their lives. If all people of God keep seeking God like they should it wouldn't be like that. Hey! Whom you yield yourselves as servants to, you obey and if you yield to the devil you're going to obey him.

CHAPTER 14

PREPARE YOURSELVES

When you're invited to a formal affair, the first thing you do is shop at the finest stores. You want to buy the finest suit or dress for that occasion. After dressing up, you make sure everything fits and is in its place. That's what we have to do, dress our soul up in the Word of God. First is getting salvation.

Since I have told you about God's Son Jesus, now I am telling you about the Epistle of (Romans 10:10) which states: *For with the heart man believeth unto righteousness; and with mouth confession is made unto salvation.* In (Romans 10:9) it states: *That if thou shalt confess with thy mouth the Lord Jesus, and shalt believe in thine heart that God hath raised him from the dead, thou shalt be saved.*

We are serving an unlimited God who has everything we need and has all that we need to make it to the Kingdom. God is for everybody, He said all souls belong to Him but the soul that sins it shall die.

Why substitute for what the enemy has to offer? He will have you leaning on your flesh and you will lose out on going back with Jesus when He comes for His Church. Put your trust in God not the arm of flesh. God is our strength and all our resources; He wants us to be strong in Him. I know at times we get lost by not obeying the Word of God. You can find yourself by seeking the Lord. In (Matthew 6:33) it states: *But seek ye first the kingdom of God, and his righteousness; and all these things shall be added unto you.* If we seek God and His righteousness He will add on to us all the spiritual things we need to survive. We're going to need it.

Find yourselves in the Word of God before the enemy finds you. You know, I've been writing this book about the "ENEMY" and I really haven't told you much about him. Let us take a closer look at him in the next chapter.

CHAPTER 15

HIS BEGINNING

B efore he became the enemy, let's take a look at the beginning of his start in the Word of the Lord. In (Ezekiel 28:13) it states: *Thou hast been in Eden the garden of God; every precious stone was thy covering, the sardius, topaz, and the diamond, the beryl, the onyx, and the jasper, the sapphire, the emerald, and the carbuncle, and gold: the workmanship of thy tabrets and of thy pipes was prepared in thee in the day that thou wast created.*

In (Ezekiel 28:14-16) it states: *Thou art the anointed cherub that covereth; and I have set thee so: thou wast upon the holy mountain of God; thou hast walked up and down in the midst of the stone of fire. Thou wast perfect in thy ways from the day that thou wast created, till iniquity was found in thee. By the multitude of thy merchandise they have filled the midst of thee with violence, and hast sinned therefore I will cast thee as profane out of the mountain of God:*

and I will destroy thee, O covering cherub, from the midst of the stone of fire.

His beginning was in Eden, the garden of God. He was a beautiful anointed cherub and perfect in his ways at that time from the day he was created. He was upon the mountain of God, "Freedom" walking up-and down in the midst of the stone of fire. God found iniquity in him. He filled the midst with violence, he sinned and God cast him out of the holy mountain. Yes, he shall be destroyed and for him there is no second chance. His heart was lifted because of his beauty. This is what caused him to become corrupted; his wisdom by reason of his brightness. God cast him out to the ground. He defiled the sanctuaries of God by all of his different kinds of the multitude of his iniquities. God said that he will bring forth a fire right in the midst of him and he's going to be destroyed. Not only that, but God's going to bring him to ashes upon the earth in the sight of everyone that beheld him. "Enemy" with his followers that went along with his program, God cast him out of the Holy Mountain.

In life if you don't maintain your anointing by praying, fasting and being watchful, you will lose out. The same thing that he did in God's Holy Mountain, the enemy brought that thing to earth with him. He will have you doing the same thing he was doing, his way and not God's way. The Scripture explains to us what he's all about.

In (Isaiah 14:12) the Bible states: *How are thou fallen from heaven, O Lucifer, son of the morning! How are thou cut down to the ground, which didst weaken the nation!*

Lucifer is more notably referred to as satan; he has weakened the nation. He is set up to do evil. He became an enemy to God and an enemy to all mankind. In (Isaiah 14:13-14) it states: *For thou hast said in thine heart, I will ascend into heaven, I will exalt my throne above the stars of God: I will sit also upon the mount of the congregation, in the sides of the north: I will ascend above the heights of the clouds; I will be like the most high.*

Our enemy planted a seed inside himself to ascend into heaven. He can't get back up there no more. Now he wants to take over God's throne so he can set up his kingdom of evil forces upon the mount of the congregation and to ascend above the heights of the clouds. He's lying to himself in what he wants to do, it will never happen. He's trying to be like God, the enemy has a takeover spirit, trying to take God's place and that's the spirit in the church today trying to take the Pastor's place. The Word of God tells us that God brought him down. The enemy caused the earth to tremble and the world to be as wilderness. God is letting us know that the enemy is the ruler of darkness and has all his demons out, the great forces of evil, out there waiting to destroy God's people. Don't let it be you.

It's time for our Lord to come any day now. Nobody knows when Jesus is coming; He's giving us enough time to prepare ourselves to go back with Him when He comes. The enemy wants to take as many as he can with him to Hell, and it's a shame, he's getting the ones in the church; and it is a shame to go to Hell from the church.

I just want to let everyone know – maybe you are aware of it – that the enemy is moving strongly in many churches. Some leaders have let their guard down giving in to the devil. He has all types of evil spirits running around. One of them is easy to identify and there are many wandering spirits and they leap like frogs at times. What they do is leap on a child of God when he or she is off guard or not watching, making them carry out whatever that spirit of the devil tells them to do; and then the spirit leaps on someone else. Now I'm not saying that Christians are possessed with spirits. What I am saying is a wandering or a leaping spirit falls on them by being unaware. Sometimes people bring them to church with them and unload them off. When you see a saint of God in the church acting strange or acting unseemly and that they are not themselves, some spirit has leaped on them and they are carrying out what that spirit tells them to do and it wanders to the next victim. The enemy has a large package with many unrighteous benefits that he is willing to pass out free of charge. He just says a few words and they "just do it."

One thing I do know is he uses people who were delivered from certain things and they're not seeking God like they used to and that spirit resurrects itself back into them. To all saints, you must stay in the church, read the Word of God, fast, pray and be watchful so that evil spirit doesn't resurrect itself back in you. Did you know that the enemy uses people's tongues to kill, back bite, and makes them to have jealousy and hate toward one another. Ever since he was cast out of heaven, he hasn't stopped planning on what's next to do to God's people. What great hatred he has for God and us. God tells us to love one another, for love is of God. Everyone that loveth is born of God and knoweth God. (1 John 4:8) states, *He that loveth not knoweth not God; for God is love.*

John 3:16 says *For God so loved the world, that he gave his only begotten son that whosoever believeth in him should not perish, but have everlasting life.* I'm glad God gave His Son to die for us. He paid it all. All we have to do is believe in the Son and receive what God has for us.

Your calling in Christ Jesus will cost you something. It's worth it all, if you are truly living according to the Word of God. He promises us eternal life. That means living with Jesus Christ forever and forever. Don't you believe it? I just want to serve you notice, you don't backslide overnight but little by little by staying away from your church family, not reading your Word and not praying, and not obeying your Pastor. And when you do decide to come to church after a long time of being away, the enemy will have you finding fault in the people in the church. He'll tell you it don't take all of that, praising God, hearing the Word of God, or staying in the church too long. That person has not the spirit of God in them. See, staying away from church you lose something that you once had when you were seeking God, and you know what? It takes that and some more. That's the devil's excuse to keep you not wanting to advance back to God. We must remember that before we gave our life to Jesus, we were a big mess, and only Christ Jesus could clean us up. The enemy doesn't want us to remember that. We were on our way to Hell. We didn't know it until someone came along and preached Jesus to us.

Many who are claiming that they are born again Christian are walking around with no understanding of the enemy, our adversary. Peter specifically identified him as the devil, someone who is trying to mess-up our life. If you never know the truth, and apply it to your life, you can never live in the fullness of the freedom that Christ purchased for us at cavalry.

I have experienced many things in my lifetime after I got saved. The enemy put some sport on me. Some I got victory over and some at that time I struggled with. I fasted and prayed for deliverance, and the Lord did just that. He delivered me. See I wanted to be delivered. The enemy doesn't care if you get victory. Yes, he will leave for a season but he is prowling around your territory waiting for a chance to ease back in. It's the same thing we go through but he comes in a different way. All those things you struggled through when you were not saved and now you are saved, but the enemy is going to bring them back. He's going to try to see if you're going to take down, or hold on to Jesus. I'm telling you to hold on to Jesus. Our God is greater and greater is He that is in you then he that is in the world.

Don't leave a door open for the devil to ease back in. When he sees you well alert, he will try another way, sometimes a push by force sending one of his high ranking officers out to try to get you. Remember, we were taken out of his hands. He's trying to get us back and he will use anything as his bait. Don't let him fool you.

I was taught how to fast, pray, stay in church and make sure my eyes were watching the enemy. He doesn't care how much you shut in the church fasting and praying. He will come right in the midst and spot you out. One thing I can say is the enemy doesn't care how much you go to church, believe God, or read the Word of God. He's there also. Sometimes we bring him along with us to church. In (James 2:19) it states: *Thou believest that there is one God; thou doest well: the devils also believe, and tremble.* The Word lets us know that the enemy believes and trembles. He can't live the Word of God. He wants to have his way and already has those in the world. We are his victims. He's targeting us. We don't have to let that be fulfilled in our life.

One of the purposes of this book is to make you aware, get tough, stand up and be strong in the Lord, so the devil (our adversary) won't do you in. Let me break this down for you so that you can understand our enemy. The word satan in Greek means the accuser: The word devil in Greek means false accuser/slanderer. The devil is our adversary. He is our opponent. The destroyer is loose on his mission seeking daily and targeting the saints of God. His reservation has been made and reserved especially for him and his followers in Hell. God did it and there is no cancelation, the enemy knows it, that's why he's working overtime blinding the mind and the eyes of the people of God if he can. I'm telling you he's trying to make things look good for you and for me to go after it.

As long as you are saved, obeying the Word of God and on your watchful post, you are on safe grounds. If you do what it takes to stay saved you will see yourself grow and grow in the

Lord. Not only that, but you will get stronger and stronger. The Word in (Ephesians 6:10) states: *Finally, my brethren be strong in the Lord, and the power of his might.* We have to do what it takes to live for the Lord. In (Romans 13:14) the Bible states: *But put on the Lord Jesus Christ, and make not provision for the flesh, to fulfil the lusts thereof.*

He is the one who accuses us and slanders you, me, and our brethren "that's our enemy." Satan's tools are out there, and cause a lot of problems in the churches. He will sow seeds of hate in the Body of Christ, and have the saints going against one another. These are the last days; the end of all things is at hand. We must be sober and watch unto prayer. The Word of God holds specific answers to all these questions. It deals with the root cause of many difficulties people currently experience in the churches. Get into the "Word of God" so you will know what time it is. The Word of God is our road map to see the Kingdom of God. The Bible tells us in (John 5:39) *Search the scriptures; for in them ye think ye have eternal life: and they are they which testify of me.*

People of God, stop being lazy and start putting on what it takes for this journey. Everyday we should get into a good habit of praying, fasting and getting into the Word of God. Before we came to Christ, we had bad habits and those bad habits came from the enemy. We were under his wings and we couldn't do anything but what he told us to do. Many people today have lost out on having salvation because they were under the wings of the enemy. So why not practice seeking the Lord and get into a habit of praying daily, fasting, and being watchful. You know the "Word of God" will dress you up in righteousness. The Word of God cleans us up, and we will bring forth fruit and grow and grow in the Lord. In order for us to grow in the Lord, we must continue in Him.

Don't disconnect yourself from the Lord. You will wither away. There are many saints that have withered away in the church because the church is not in them and I'm not talking about a building. We are the church. We that are strong in the Lord need to help those who are trying to find their way back and those who the enemy has tricked. If you can't do nothing but pray, the Lord answers prayer.

All the problems the enemy causes in our life, we shouldn't let that remain. It's correction time. Get it right and don't let the sun go down on you. There's work to be done outside the church. Lots of souls – some hurting because of mess the enemy used against them while they were unwatchful.

Tell pride it has to go!!! Invite humbleness into your heart, I believe obeying God will follow forgiveness. If you hurt anyone go to that person and tell them to forgive you for your wrong doing. Where are you going if you cannot forgive? There are a lot of church people walking around singing songs of Zion, praising God, shouting, speaking in tongues that have hurt their sisters and brothers in Christ. Some of them are preachers. We have to be very careful when we talk and how we talk. That's the devil's doing. That tongue is something else. When James wrote the Epistle of James, he talked about the tongue and how it is a little member and it boasts out great things. He goes on to say the tongue is a fire a world of iniquity, the tongue will defile our whole body and no man can tame the tongue. It is unruly evil. Only God can tame our tongue.

Don't let the enemy use you in hurting your sisters and brothers, and if you are caught up like that get with the one you have hurt and talk about it. Go and apologize to them. There is too much division, unforgiveness, and pride going on in the church. That needs to stop. We are the children of the day, we have to love one another. Don't give space to the enemy; not even an inch. Put the Word on him.

Many today have let the enemy turn the place of worship into a playhouse without God's presence. In its changes the territory of saints become the territory of satan. Last days holiness of the saints has ceased to be what it stands for. The light of the truth and the love they had for God has failed because the enemy has stepped into the church. The Kingdom influence of salt has lost its savor. God's Word has been replaced by man's wisdom and God's way has been replaced by man's desire. Whatever the enemy planted in them their worship has become vain. Yet and still, they think what they are doing is right even when they were committed to God, they replaced it with compromise and have turned back to vanity and pride when they used to have victory over sin. We are serving a God that loves us in the midst of letting the enemy rob us. In (Revelation 3:20) it states: *Behold I stand at the door, and knock: if any man hear my voice, and open, I will come in to him, and will sup with him, and he with me.*

The churches have put Jesus outside of their lives and He is standing there knocking, He wants to come back in. He loves us, but there is a problem there. The enemy has the churches in a place where they can't open up for Christ to come in. All Jesus wants is to have a followership service with them that He loves. The Bible says in Revelation that they were not hot or cold, they were lukewarm. Our churches today have turned cold, too cold to open up and let God come back into them. A church without God encounters the judgment of God in severity and that's a serious problem.

As you read this book take salvation seriously and think about this when you go to worship service: *What am I here for? Am I here just to say I went to church or I am here to give my life to the Lord and to live for Him or do I just want to stay in the arms of the enemy?*

Time is short and too short for anybody who wants to wait until later or to play around with the enemy.

CHAPTER 16

GO ALL THE WAY

Once you get it together there's always room for more of Jesus. Don't be like the sons of the Prophets in Bethel (House of God). They were just there taking it easy maybe holding a title as the sons of the prophets. I don't know, but I do know they saw a man of God going forward to obtain his calling in the Lord. They were used by the enemy trying to discourage Elisha along his journey. Elisha's mind was made up to go all the way. I believe Elisha wanted to tell them to shut up but he didn't. When the sons of the Prophets told him that his master would be taken away from him, Elisha told them, I know it. Hold your peace. Elisha didn't want to hear anything they had to say.

There are people who don't care if you make it or not. Many today their mind is open for them to be used by the enemy. You who have started with the Lord, I'm telling you to go all the way. (Matthew 10:22) states, *And ye shall be hated of all men for my name's sake: but he that endureth to the end shall be saved.* Keep on going and see what the end is going to be and if you are found in The "Word of God" you know where you are headed. If you have repented and have Christ on board, you will be with the Lord.

I believe Elijah the man of God often talked to Elisha his son in the Lord. Like a father and son talk, since Elijah experienced a lot of the enemy's attacks. Maybe Elijah asked Elisha, "Are you willing to seek the face of God with me? Are you willing to pay the price of listening and obeying the voice of God? Will you learn of His Word and His ways? Walking in God's perfect will or will you choose to take the easy road that the other prophets are taking?" The Word is for us today. Are you willing to seek God's face, to listen, to obey the voice of the Lord, to learn His Word and His ways, and are you willing to pay the price whatever it take to go all the way or do you want the enemy to tell you it don't take all of that and that he will show you a quick and easy way?

Elijah told Elisha to stay here at the beginning right at Gilgal. The question is asking us the same things. Are we willing to do what it takes to live and to do work for the Lord? Just as we see often in our day and time, if a man or woman of God makes a total commitment to God, there's always a person who the enemy will use to try to make you take down. To me the sons of the prophets had an attitude toward

Elisha or couldn't see him advancing himself forward in the Lord. They felt inferior and if the sons of the prophets were seeking like Elisha was, they wouldn't be standing looking at the man of God advancing his life in God, getting all that he can for the great work before him.

God was preparing Elisha. The sons of the prophets didn't see it. They couldn't catch the vision. The enemy was using them to attempt to bring Elisha down to their level of commitment of doing nothing but watching the people of God going on with their lives. This is what they said to Elisha "Why are you following Elijah? Don't you know he's almost finished?" They wanted to know why? The enemy has put the sons of the prophets to sleep. There are many Christians today that have been rocked to sleep by the devil. They are carrying the name of Christ saying they are Christian. Some are carrying titles, saying they have been called by God, but not the character which should go with the name. Yes, God was in their life but somehow or another, the cares of this life pushed Christ out of their life. They show no faith just walking by sight and the enemy lets them see what he wants them to see and when he gets you in a spot like that, it's all about the enemy and his plans for you.

Elisha's decision to follow Elijah was not a one-time decision. After every part of the journey Elisha was challenged by Elijah whether he would continue on the journey or find a place of comfort and stay there. Elijah knew that it would not only take commitment and dedication but it would take perseverance in the face of discouragement. That's where the enemy comes in to discourage us while we are on our journey; sometimes through others or within. Somehow or another he's on his mission to steal us, destroys us and kill, and to carry us with him. He doesn't care how he does it as long as he has us. Think! Why? Can't we be on our mission for God living holy out in the field winning men and women to Christ? Now we see that Elisha let nothing stop him. By him going all the way he saw a supernatural miracle. God took Elijah into heaven, and Elijah's ministry was handed down to Elisha. Elisha wore Elijah's mantle because he stayed by the man of God and didn't let nothing hinder him. Your walk with Christ is very serious. Don't let the enemy hinder you.

CHAPTER 17

HE GOT YOU

The enemy has people as free agents going from church to church finding others to join in with them that are like them. "Miserable" they love company, living their own life style. Asleep, thinking they are alright. Not so. God is holy and this is a holy way.

The enemy's got you sleep walking and spiritually dead. He blindfolds the eyes and mind. He will have your soul in awful peril and you will be lost. Did you not know you're going to be judged? We have to prepare ourselves to meet God. If you haven't prepared yourself, it's time for change and your heart needs to be renewed. You are headed the wrong way. The Bible in (Romans 6:23) states *For the wages of sin is death; but the gift of God is eternal life through Jesus Christ our Lord.*

There are many today who don't understand that we all have sinned and come short of the glory. We thank God for His Son Jesus Christ obeying His Father by coming down to die for us. Sin separated us from God. The enemy caused all of that, but we thank God for Jesus.

I'm addressing this to all of God's people – Stop being lazy. Put on what it takes for this journey. Everyday we must seek the Lord and dress up in His Word, that's what cleans us up, (John 15:3) states: *Now ye are clean through the word which I have spoken unto you.* It is good when the Word of God gets a hold on you. There is a change. We bear fruit because we are connected to the main source, the Vine. If we disconnect ourselves from the Lord, we will wither away. Today many have withered away from God because the enemy has fooled them. Some are in the church but the church is not in them. We who really have what it takes, let us pray for those that the Lord will deliver them.

Wake-up!! Wake-up!! What time is it? Inventory yourselves. All the problems that the enemy causes in your life, they can't remain. You must correct them. Don't let the sun go down on you. There's work to be done outside the church. Lots of souls, some have been hurting because of mess inside the church and extra stuff the enemy threw on them. They are trying to get out but the enemy has rocked them to sleep while they were caught off guard not being watchful.

You can be in the Lord, in the church for years, and years. The enemy doesn't care. I have seen where un-watchful saints got caught off guard. He will put you to sleep and start many activities in your mind. Before you know it, he has ripped you off of everything you have had in Christ Jesus.

Whether you know it or not, that's another one of his missions. Don't even think you got it made. I guess Samson thought he had it made. One thing Samson did that we find ourselves doing is playing around with the enemy. He knows the weakest part in us all and he will take that and play a game with you just like he did Samson. See, Samson loved women and that's what the enemy used to bring him down. When Samson came to himself it was too late, he lost what he had. The enemy put sport on him and blinded him. In the midst of it all he prayed to God to restore him. God restored Him but he lost his life. Samson was a Nazirite set apart to God from birth. Oh yes he was the one to begin the deliverance of Israel from the hands of the Philistines. The enemy let his flesh rise up and took control because he played the enemy's game. It took death to get the job done.

Don't let the enemy play with your life. When you get caught in any problems, it might not be like Samson, but it could be anything that is wrong or interferes with your walk with Christ. You got to get rid of it before it gets rid of you. Samson relaxed himself in the arms of the enemy and when the announcement went forward letting him know that his enemy is upon him, he shook himself and nothing happened. While he was relaxing in the arms of the enemy, the devil took all his strength. We who are in Christ Jesus must continue to seek the Lord and don't let the devil put us in a relaxed mode, then he will start speaking the things we liked to do before we came to Christ, then it sounds good to us, he lets whatever he puts in our mind linger much, that's the seed he plants in our mind then it starts travelling to the heart. You can't stay like that. The problem must be corrected.

We who are claiming salvation, saying that we are saved and set aside for the Master's use, many people are watching us. They don't really want to hear a sermon. They want to see you live what you're talking about. Those who are looking for a better way of living who have tried everything are looking toward the church, and we must be that perfect example. But many Churches today have let the people down by living any kind of way. In other words they saying one thing and living like the world.

Many people are hurting from bad experiences, and some of them used to be in the church, where they were mistreated, put down, talked about, and lied on. It's not good to be in the church and get church hurt, the church should be like a hospital where there is healing, Where the Word of God is being preached and having its full course. Many saints of God are giving up because of church hurt over nonsense,

HE GOT YOU

and over he said. she said mess. Foolishness needs to be cut down by the Word of God in the church. It's time out for all that junk the enemy is handing out. You'd be surprised at the ones that the enemy is using. They have been in church for years; some of them singing in the choir, on the usher board, shouting every time church music plays, the ones receiving the offering, *and* them gifted ones.

We are living in the days where the enemy is running some of the churches, he has his followers taking over and putting his program on the list, running the church like he wants it to be. He doesn't like prayer, fasting and the Word of God. The enemy is a problem, a big problem. He targets any and everything that he can use. If you're not on your watchful post, he's on the way to check you out to see how much he can use you to do wrong things.

We who are saved don't give space for the devil – not even an inch. If you give the enemy some space he will fill you up with all kinds of his junk that's not of God. You will be bound and he will have you thinking you're okay. You are not okay. You need to be set free. The Bible in (John 8:36) states, *If the Son therefore shall make you free, ye shall be free indeed.* The enemy, when he speaks, it's a lie. He speaks of his own, for he is a liar and the father of it. In (John 8: 32) it states *And ye shall know the truth, and the truth shall make you free.*

99

In order for us to grow in the Lord, we must stay in the Word of God. There is nothing hidden from God, He sees everything. All things are naked and open unto the eyes of Him. In other words all things lie openly exposed before His eyes. Remember, God was talking to Adam in the Garden of Eden in the book of Genesis. First, He called unto Adam and said unto him, "Where art thou?" God sees and knows. He was waiting for an answer from Adam. Adam said, "I heard your voice in the garden, and I was afraid because I was naked: and I hid myself." God saw Adam and God said to Adam, "Who told you that you were naked?" God knew that the enemy was there in the midst sowing his seeds of disobedience.

God asked Adam, "Hast you eaten off the tree that I told you not to eat?" God told man he could eat of every tree in the garden freely, but of the tree of the knowledge of good and evil, God told him not to eat of it saying: "for the day that you eat, you shall surely die." And that's what happened. We need to listen to the right and good things. The enemy always points us in the wrong direction, and when we wake up it's too late. Adam told God, "It's that woman you gave me and she gave me of the tree and I did eat." In life we're always blaming somebody else, so God asked the woman, "What is this you have done?" And the woman blamed the serpent. She said he beguiled her and she ate. When it came down to the serpent the Lord God said unto him, "Because of what you've done, thou art cursed above all cattle, and every beast of the field; upon your belly you're going to crawl and eat dust all the days of your life." That's what happened to the serpent. So we have an enemy right in the midst of us each and every day.

We must stay in the Word daily and we must apply it to our life. The Word of God searches us out. That's our contact with God. We are convicted by the Word. I look at it like a threefold conviction, The Word convicts us of our union with satan; of judgment because the prince of this world is judged; that the natural man is judged in satan and is a child of satan. The Word convicts of righteousness showing that although we are children of the devil, righteousness is available and belongs to us. The Word convicts of sin because we believe not on Him. There is only one sin for which the sinner will be judged; that is the rejection of Jesus Christ.

We are recreated by the Word; the Word brought us forth. (James 1:18) states: *Of his own will begat he us with the word of truth, that we should be a kind of firstfruits of his creatures.* Any time the enemy wants to play tricks with you, put the Word on him. Let him know that you've been born again not of corruptible seed, but of incorruptible by the Word of God which liveth and abideth forever.

The Word imparts to us eternal life. If it was not for the Word, we would not know that there was a redemption or a substitution or a new creation. (2 Corinthians 5:17-18) states: *Therefore if any man be in Christ, he is a new creature: old things are passed away; behold, all things are become new. All things are of God, who hath reconciled us to himself by Jesus Christ, and hath given to us the ministry of reconciliation;*

CHAPTER 18

RENEW YOURSELF DAILY

Our minds are renewed by the Word, by being transformed, then we can prove what is that good and acceptable, and perfect, will of God. There is a change in our lives and we are no longer conformed to this world, we are living in this world but not of it. We have put on the new man which is renewed in knowledge after the image of Him that created us. Renewed by studying the Word of God, by acting upon it – we can study the Word of God for years and if we don't act upon it, live it or be a doer of the Word, then we need to check and see if the enemy has slipped in by us not being watchful.

God gave us everything we need in the Word of God. If we let the Word abide, the Word begins to take root in us. The Word will become valuable to us because we are letting the Word be all of our life. (Ephesians 3:17) states: *That Christ may dwell in your hearts by faith; ye, being rooted and grounded in love,* (so let the word of God have the right-of-way in your life.)

One thing I can say is that we need to get established, that means to settle; make stable or firm, to introduce and cause to grow and multiple, to bring into existence, and other meanings. We as saints of God need to settle down, stop going from church to church, and find a church home so that we can grow in the Lord.

God has no pleasure in weak and feeble children. Now God loves them and will care for them, shield and protect them, but has no joy in it. God is looking for someone who is willing to take a stand, to grow, have faith, someone to be strong when the storm, wind and the rain of life hits. You can have the Word ready for the enemy when he comes. God provided strength and grace for us. All of us as believers owe it to ourselves to be established in the Word. That means we'd be settled, fixed and we wouldn't be carried away by every storm, wind and rain. We'd be no more children tossed to and fro and carried about with every wind of doctrine, by the sleight of men, and cunning craftiness, whereby they lie in wait to deceive. Those who have been carried away with every wind of doctrine, the enemy has them. We who are in Christ Jesus by now should know what to stand for and who we are standing for.

CHAPTER 19

GOD LAID THE FOUNDATION

Did you know that you have been chosen before the foundation of the world and that we should be holy and without blame before Christ in love? We have redemption through His blood, the forgiveness of sins according to the riches of His grace.

We should know what Christ means to us. We have been established in righteousness through Him. We have the nature and the life of God. In the Word (John 6:47) states: V*erily, verily, I say unto you, He that believeth on me hath everlasting life.* Eternal life is the nature of the Father, and we have that now. He said He is the bread of life. We have the righteousness of God in Christ Jesus. There're few people who are established, few appreciate or understand it or have ever entered into its fullness because they let the enemy steal it from them. We are being established in grace, and what is grace? Unmerited favor of God. It is love pouring itself out upon the graceless and the unworthy. You see, grace is love in operation. God put His love beyond doubt in that while we were yet sinners Christ died for us. He made a way for us to escape out of the hands of the enemy.

Tell me what more can God do? He has laid the foundation and opened up a way for you and I, and His foundation is the core of every true believer known only to God. (2 Timothy 2:19) states *Nevertheless the foundation of God standeth sure, having this seal, The Lord knoweth them that are his. And, let every one that nameth the name of Christ depart from iniquity.*

It's time to make a departure and give the enemy all his junk back. Let him keep it and take it where he's headed. You don't need any of his baggage. If you accept just a little of what he has to offer, that's your start in preparing you to go where he is headed. Don't let him speak to you, and if you listen, he's going to pack you with a lot of his stuff and have a good time in your life. As a reminder, he is out on his mission. His mission is not a good one. He's out to kill, steal and to destroy. We see the signs of the times in what he is doing to people. Killing is very high, young and old in the natural and he's using people to kill the saints of God with their tongue.

The enemy comes to churches trying to destroy the works of God and the lives of the saints, and stealing, making the saints feel like

God is not real, showing them there is a better way out than living for the Lord. He will show you something so desirable that it will tempt you to go after it. And after you have put down all the good things that the Lord has given you for some trash the enemy offers you, he'll be standing there laughing at you. Could you think just for a moment and say to yourself, *I let the enemy make a fool out of me.*

Well there were two sons in the Bible, the younger one asked his father for his portion of his goods and so his father divided unto them his living. This younger son took a journey into a far country and spent up everything that he had. The enemy had him wasting his substance with riotous living. Everything he had was gone. Hard times hit. There rose a famine in that land. No one would help him after he spent all his money on them. He went job hunting and he found one, but he had to become a citizen of that country in order to get a job. This son was hungry and the job he got was feeding pigs. The enemy brought him down way low from the way he was living. When he went to do his job feeding pigs, the bucket he had in his hand that he began to pour the food for the pigs it looked good to him and he began to bend down to eat. (Luke 15: 17) states *And when he came to himself, he said, How many hired servants of my father's have bread enough and to spare, and I perish with hunger!*

107

The young son made up his mind that he was going to go back to his father and say, "Father I have sinned against heaven and before thee," and he felt like he was not worthy to be his son. The father had love for his son, was praying for his son and was glad to see his son return back home.

That's just like God who loves us so much He doesn't want any of us lost. That's why He sent His son to come to die on the cross so that we can be reconciled back to Him. Sin separates us from God.

The enemy is the cause of that, and now he's working on the other elder son that never left home. When he heard all the music inside of the house, he called and asked one the servants what was going on inside the house, so the servant told him, "Your brother done came home. Your father has killed the fatted calf because he has received him safe and sound." So the devil jumped into him and he was angry and would not go in. His father came out and entreated him. He told his father, "Lo all these many years did I serve thee; neither transgressed I at any time thy commandment; but you never gave me a kid that I might make merry with my friends. As soon as your son came home, from the streets living with harlots, you killed the best fatted calf." The father told his elder son, "You have always been with me and all that I have is yours."

We have to be careful how we treat people in the church and also the ones that come back to the Lord; Even if you have never left the church. That's one of the enemy's tricks. He will turn us against one another having us walking around mad with one another. The father told him it was "meet that we should make merry, and be glad: for this thy brother was dead, and is alive again; and was lost and is found." Heaven rejoices when one soul comes to Christ and gets saved.

Nobody's mad but the devil, and let him stay mad. He can't do anything about it but stay out of God's way. We serve a mighty God, an all powerful God who has the whole world in His hands. I'm telling everyone who's reading this book, value your time, stay in the Word of God, stay prayed up and fasted up. Above all, stay on your watchful post. Throughout this book I repeat myself on certain things, like being watchful, prayer, fasting, the devil, and satan so don't take it lightly; take it to heart. You are going to need it when you go through some things.

I'm writing to all born again believers, also for those who've been in the church for years. Those that have been there for years, sometimes they don't know what's going on in the church and some do know. Could you imagine that you are in the church service praising God and all of a sudden the enemy comes in the midst changing the whole service around? I remember in this church, praise service was going on and these three people walked in the church doors with the enemy's helper ushering them. You could feel the force of evil. The Deacon began to look around and didn't know what to say or sing next. He was speechless because the spirit of the devil came in the doors of the church and robbed the people of their praise service. That's why we have to be watchful. I told you early in this book that the enemy said he wants to be like the "Most High." He's trying to be what he's not.

Many saints today haven't experienced the spirit of the devil. When they see a spirit move, they think it's God. What did the Bible say? (1John 4:1) states: *Beloved, believe not every spirit, but try the spirits whether they are of God: because many false prophets are gone out into the world.*

The devil comes to church with you. I know you're thinking and saying to yourself, *what does she mean?* Well, when you come to church when it's praise and worship time and when you see yourself just sitting there doing nothing, not giving what's due unto the Lord. God wants us to praise Him. We come to church to worship the Lord. In the Book of (Psalms 147:1) it states *Praise ye the Lord: for it is good to sing praises unto our God; for it is pleasant; and praise is comely.* In the book of Psalms, it's all about praising God. There are some that do praise God, get their dance in, but when it's time for the Word of God, they start yawning because they are tired from dancing, clock watching, then they go to the bathroom, and some have a conversation while the preacher is preaching. These are the ones that bring the devil to church with them. They be thinking *I'll be glad when the service finish cause I got things to do.* That's the enemy speaking to them because he's in the midst of the service blocking them from hearing the Word of God. They brought that spirit, maybe from home, to church; or they attach and cling to them when they're on their way into the church. I do know the enemy will have his spirits clinging to you unawares.

To all saved people, mainly the preacher, when the Pastor goes forth to deliver the message to the congregation, you all need to be standing behind him or her with prayer that the Word of God be delivered to the people. When you see souls getting saved, blessed and healed, you know that the Word is taking its full course. Some churches are caught up in tradition. They are not scriptural. You have to be careful with that because the enemy will change your program and tell you it doesn't take all that fasting, praying reading and teaching the Word of God. He will speak to you through someone else and tell you it don't take all that going to church all the time, you can tell that person that's talking to you it takes all of that and some more. The enemy wants us to reverse or do the opposite of what the Word of God tells us to do. My Bible tells me in (Ephesians 4:27) where it states: *Neither give place to the devil.* Sometimes we unawares give the devil place especially when we play around his territory. We stop doing the things that we're supposed to do like reading the Word of God and applying it to our lives, and seeking God on a daily basis. The enemy is trying to put us out of business in seeking God. I told you before he wants us to seek him, not God. Satan wants to be like God. He's making a mess with himself and trying to make a mess with us. His time is running out.

CHAPTER 20

THE ENEMY HAS NOTHING TO OFFER

The Spirit of God dwells on the inside of us. We have been renewed in the spirit of our mind since we have put on the new man which is after God that is created in righteousness and in true holiness. It's time for a check-up and clean-up. Give the enemy all his tools. Everything unrighteous belongs to him. You don't have to do what the enemy tells you to do. When you get saved, you exchange bosses and Jesus rules in your life.

Tell the enemy that you belong to the Lord. Sometimes we let the enemy bring things that we put to death back to life. We all are guilty and don't say I don't know what I'm talking about. Anytime when you stop reading The Word of God, stop praying, stop going to church, and stop being around your church family, something is wrong there. The enemy has you making excuses about some of everything. To serve you notice, all excuses went to the cross with Christ.

The devil will say you can pray at home, it don't take all that church going, you're going to get sick fasting and a lot of other things he will say to you, and that's his job. That's how he hinders us from getting all the benefits we need from God.

We all know what God delivered us from. We were in a rough situation where only God could deliver us. You, I and a lot of others were in a messed up state where only God could help us. So don't even let the enemy speak or put a thought in your mind. Get up from there. Stop holding on to the devil's junk. Clean yourself up and stop carrying his baggage around. He has nothing good to offer. His tools are dangerous, and if you play around and get a hold of just one of his tools you might not be able to get rid of it. His tools deal with sin and sin is death. See, he knows what he's doing and I have a question for you. Do you know what you are doing? Letting him (the enemy) have space in your life?

You who are saved, don't let the enemy trick you because if he tricks, the treat is not good. Let us lay aside the weight and the sin that will easily beset us, we are in a race and let us run with patience the race that's set before us. Look to Jesus, He is the author and finisher of our faith (not unto the enemy but unto Jesus).

The tools of the enemy are on his table spread out for you to use and especially when you are going through. He makes it look very tempting along with his lies he tells. He treats you to all his lies that he tells you by giving you his promise. He doesn't have a promise, but God gave him His Word, in (Revelation 20:11) it states *And the devil that deceived them was cast into the lake of fire and brimstone, where the beast and the false prophet are, and shall be tormented day and night for ever and ever.*

See he's on his way out. Don't be no fool and be in the number with him. Don't play around with him. If you do, I am telling you that you are headed for a life sentence with him and that is death. Take heed to the things I am telling you. Don't let it slip at anytime. Stay in the Word of God and grow. In (Hebrews 2:3) it states *How shall we escape, if we neglect so great salvation; which at the first began to be spoken by the Lord, and was confirmed unto us by them that heard him;*

I'm telling you all who are in Christ Jesus stay with life, don't fool with death. God offers us everlasting life through His Son, Jesus Christ our Lord, and the wages of sin is death. I have another question, what's so great that the enemy has to offer that you want to be with him? My answer is, the enemy has nothing to offer you and me, and he wants to share his evilness so he can have him some company in Hell with him. I'm not going to say sitting in Hell because you won't have time for that. You're going to be tormented forever. I have talked to many people today about salvation. Some of them like their lifestyle without Christ. I explain to them about Jesus, His death, His burial and resurrection. Many will tell you they know Jesus, they go to church, but they can't give you an answer that they repented of the sins and accepted the Lord Jesus as Lord and savior in their life.

We have God's good Word so that we can make it into the Kingdom of heaven, and it's a shame that we're saying okay but dragging our feet. The time is now to get salvation. We are quick to listen to the devil more than listen to what will bail us out of sin. God gave us what we need and a warning also in the Word of God. He doesn't want any of us lost, that's just like God. His love is everlasting to everlasting. Choose life not death

CHAPTER 21

GOD IS IN CONTROL

We must keep in mind that God is in control, not satan. The enemy can't do more than what God allows him to do. Yes, we all have wilderness experiences in our lives and at times it hits hard. If we are anchored in Jesus, we will get the victory. God gave us what we need, and our offensive weapon that we possess is the sword of the spirit which is the Word of God. Now you know we have His Word to carry us through, and when you're going through don't complain like the children of Israel.

Let God get the glory out of your life. Stay in the Word of God; recognize temptation and resist the devil and he will flee from you, but he will be back and try you again and again. This will go on until Jesus comes back and raptures His church.

The most important thing is to know the Word of God and be able to use the Word when the enemy comes.

Don't let nobody tell you that Jesus is not real, He's real. I know He is. You who have never been saved, first you must recognize that you are a sinner and you are in need of a savior and that you cannot save yourself. Then repent and turn from you sins. All those who have gone to sleep, wake up and come back to the Lord.

God knows all about you. He knows what you've been through and He knows what you're going through now. It's good when you have and know a good God that sees and knows all things. He knows our down sitting and our up-rising, our beginning and our end, every string of hair on our head, He knows. He saw you when the road got tough and you turned back and went back into the world because the enemy filled you up with his junk and then laughed and left you hanging. All God wants you to do is come, return unto him. He will not keep his anger forever, for God is merciful and a longsuffering God. In (Jeremiah 3:14) it states: *Turn, o backsliding children, saith the Lord; for I am married unto you: and I will take you one of a city, and two of a family, and I will bring you to zion.* God's Word is true. Don't let the enemy fool you. A lot of people who once knew the Lord fooling around with the devil have backslidden. They went back out into the world wandering and can't find their way back.

God will give you a pastor according to His heart, which shall feed you with knowledge and understanding. I am talking about a pastor who has been set aside and dedicated, living Holy unto the Lord; the one that passed the test. Jesus passed the test. Remember a voice from heaven saying, "This is my beloved Son, in whom I am well pleased." After this marvelous experience, Jesus was led by the Spirit into the wilderness to be tempted by the devil, but Jesus got the victory. God is using those kinds of pastors, who are walking upright before Him, not taking down but getting victory. God wants His people saved and to be blessed.

God will balance our life. Even when we go through the mountain top, the valley or the wilderness experiences, God is there. We need to be especially alert when we've gone through a great spiritual experience because the enemy is waiting for his opportunity. This is true of many of the Old Testament heroes, No sooner had Elijah taken care of the false prophets on Mount Carmel then he was so discouraged he wanted to die. There were times in the lives of Jeremiah and Moses when they wanted to quit.

The enemy knows when we've had an emotional or spiritual experience. He knows where to get us the most. Remember he had us before, so he is standing on guard to attack us again. Our attacker never gives up and never gives in. He's on his post trying to defeat us. but not so. We are in Christ Jesus. We are the head and not the tail. We have victory in Christ Jesus our Lord. So hold on to God's unchanging hand. It won't be long until all this will be over. Thank you Jesus.

You may wonder why Christ was tempted by the devil. It may seem odd that Jesus was led by the Holy Spirit into the wilderness to be tempted by Satan. But God had a very definite purpose for allowing His Son to be tested in this way, and I can think of some reasons. One of them is to prepare Him. God the Father was preparing God the Son to be our sympathetic, understanding High Priest. Christ knows exactly what we are going through because He endured the same temptations, frustrations, and sufferings. Jesus knows our struggles. He will guide and keep us. He's our friend.

The second reason: to expose the enemy. Satan was now waiting for Jesus. The devil doesn't want you or me to know what his tactics are. I'm talking about his skillful plans. When we realize that he is tempting us, we are much more capable of resisting him. So he lurks in the darkness and disguises his temptation so we will be deceived into sinning. He knows if he can keep us in the dark it will be a much easier time holding us in bondage.

I believe this event in the wilderness dragged the enemy out of the darkness into the light. This way all his tactics could be exposed. The key to winning or getting victory is we must get to know the battle plans of the enemy. God allowed Jesus to be tempted so he could expose satan's battle plan. When we understand the methods the enemy used in tempting Jesus, we will better understand how he works and how to put the Word of God on the enemy. Don't let the enemy drag you from the light back into darkness. You know Judas Iscariot, along with the other disciples, was around the table with the light. Jesus said, "One of you shall betray me." Everyone began to ask, *Lord is it I?* Jesus said he that dippeth his hand with me in the dish, the same shall betray me. The enemy had Judas Iscariot. He asked Jesus, "Master is it I?" Jesus told him, "You have said it." What I'm saying is the enemy left the darkness came into the light and entered into Judas, and Judas left the light and went into darkness to betray Jesus. Why Judas one of Jesus followers? Judas did not have to let that be fulfilled in his life. It should have been someone else for Scripture to be fulfilled. This lets us know that the enemy doesn't care. He will use whoever is available, even someone close to you. The enemy is all about darkness. There is no light whatsoever in him. His deeds are very evil.

The third is to teach us. See Jesus was tempted by Satan so He could expose his tactics to us in order to teach us the way to victory. Christ is our example of how to stand firm in the face of temptation. Jesus didn't face the enemy with his divine power. He faced him as a man relying on the Spirit of God and the Word of God with Him. Jesus was tempted in every way that we will also be tempted, but he (Jesus) did not sin. Adam disobeyed and fell into sin. We have inherited a sinful nature. Jesus Christ became a man in order to show us how to rise above that nature. The temptations Jesus faced and conquered were much more severe than what Adam succumbed to. For example, Adam was tempted in a beautiful garden while the Lord Jesus Christ was tempted in the barren wilderness.

Adam had all kinds of food at his fingertips, yet he deliberately chose to eat the one fruit that God had forbidden. On the other hand, Jesus had not eaten in 40 days and 40 nights. Adam failed to resist a small temptation, plunging the entire human race into sin and death. To serve you notice, the enemy was there.

Look at Jesus. He succeeded in living a sinless life, offering us salvation and eternal life. We can live Holy unto the Lord, what the first man Adam didn't do, the second man Adam came along and showed us that we can live righteous unto the Lord. We have everything in The Word of God. Start reading your Word and stop letting God's Word collect dust on the bookshelf. Pull it down, and read. Study and get the Word into you so you can grow in Christ Jesus. God is looking for strong and bold soldiers in His army; someone who can take a stand in these last days. Don't let the devil stop or block your progress in the Lord.

CHAPTER 22

USING OUR SINFUL NATURE

Often you and I have a tendency to use our sinful nature as an excuse for giving into temptation. First thing he will have us to say is *I'm only human* or *I can't help it if my sinful nature keeps getting the best of me.* I have heard others say *God knows I can't be perfect.* When we are like that, we are lacking something and that's the Word of God. We have the same resources at our disposal that our Lord used when He met satan, and that is the Word. Resist him. Watch out.

The enemy will mess with us physically. You're praying asking God for a wife or husband and while you're praying you believe and wait on God but on the other hand, the enemy speaks to your mind or through someone else and they tell you that you're not getting any younger, go out and find you somebody; or they will say enjoy life while you're here in this life. Just go and satisfy your needs. God understands. This was once said to me and they added, "You only have one life to live." Listen. If I had obeyed what was said to me while I'm walking in the light and turned around to go into darkness shopping for my lustful needs, and if Jesus had come back I would lose out and in Hell I would lift up my eyes being tormented. Dealing emotionally sometimes, we get sick in the body, family have problems, or death or other things happen. That's where the enemy plays with our emotions. We get sad, we weep and have pain, but in the midst of it all, we should be looking to Jesus. Spiritually, the enemy will take advantage of our weakened physical condition and attack us. He always tries to find ways to attack us. These things I just mentioned I have been through some of them all.

The enemy doesn't want us to be spiritual. That's why he throws these attacks on us. He will tell us, *you can't live spiritual all the time.* He will put in our mind that our physical needs are on the line. I serve you notice in this book; it is impossible to separate the physical from the spiritual. Our body, soul, and spirit work together to make us the person we are. And what affects one part, also affects the whole. The way we use our bodies affect's our spiritual lives. Your emotions affect your physical body. Be careful what you allow your mind to dwell on. That will affect your emotions. When you try to separate the physical from the spiritual, it eventually leads to sin and that's what the enemy wants. Look at it this way; the enemy has many strongholds, and if we're not careful those imagination thoughts will come and if you dwell on them, he will make them come alive. I know you are saying what does she mean? Well, the enemy can invent a great imagination in your mind. He will take you to fairyland, and have you picking the things up again that you have put away. It only takes a little entertaining of what he has worked up in your mind. Then you give in, indulge to the enemy and you have created something bigger than you could handle. Again I tell you those are his darts.

Have you ever wanted something real bad and you do all you can to get it? And you don't stop unto you get it? It could be something no good for you, but you want it; something not going to help you, but you got to have it; is not a life time thing, but you want it. What about wanting Jesus? He's everlasting, has all you need, and is full of peace, joy, happiness and freedom. God has everything we need. Just trust him. Keep on living for it won't be long. The time is ticking just like a clock. God wants what's best for His people. He made a way for the children of Israel. He heard them when they were in Egypt. God had a plan to set them free. He raised up Moses right among them to deliver them out of Egypt. God sent His Son to die for you and me but we still don't get it. Just like the children of Israel. When Moses did all he could do for God's people, they let the enemy use them against him. Moses cried unto the Lord and asked the Lord what he should do unto this people; they were ready to stone him. The Lord stepped in and told Moses to "Go on before the people and take with thee the elders of Israel; and thy rod." and told him to smite the rock with the rod. He did and out came water that the people may drink. Moses did so in the sight of the elders, they saw the miracles of God.

Moses had a lot on his hands. He was dealing with self-appointed, self-righteous proud men. Their reasoning was a deceptive and dangerous form of rebellion and that's one of the enemy's tools and that's his way of making you fall into his traps. When you have a good leader and God is using him or her, the enemy doesn't like that. The enemy will do all he can to start something in the church. When the people wanted to rise up against Moses and Aaron, God became so angry He wanted to destroy all of them. But Aaron and Moses interceded for the people. A plague broke out from the Lord, which killed fourteen thousand and seven hundred people. Let me warn you. It's not good to be rebellious. God doesn't like it. He hates it. When our enemy Lucifer rebelled, God did not ask him to leave. He was thrown out as fast as lightning falls from the sky to earth. (Luke 10:18) states *And he said unto them, I beheld Satan as lightning fall from heaven.*

Finally, Moses' sister and brother went against him. They complained to God about the Ethiopian woman Moses married. The biggest problem was a jealous and proud spirit, because they said, "Has the Lord indeed spoken only by Moses? Has he not spoken also by us?" When we are family, the enemy will come in to divide, confuse us and cause us to fight among ourselves. The issue wasn't about the woman he married or about God using Moses. Self got in the way. They had been with their brother all that time and now they were letting the enemy use them. Be careful what you say. God will hear you. What they did, it didn't go so well because they spoke against the man of God. God punished Miriam with leprosy and she had to stay outside the camp for a week. They couldn't move forward. Her cause held them back until she could come back inside the camp. Just like sin – it will separate us from the love of God and sin is not going into heaven.

Pride and murmuring are two of the enemy's powerful tools, See, it attacked two of Moses family members; and when it attacks a large group of people it causes great damage. It affects everyone. Remember when God told Moses to send the spies out, one of every tribe to search the land and when they returned from searching the land, ten brought back an evil report and the enemy attacked everyone in the camp who didn't have faith but operated in doubt and fear. They murmured against Moses and it caused some to die in the wilderness. The enemy is happy when things happen like that. We have to watch out and don't use, take or borrow the enemy's tools. Don't even dwell on them and if you do, he will try to set up a workshop in your mind. If he does, it goes to the heart and you will be doing everything he tells you to do because you gave birth to whatever he put in your mind. He set up the workshop; now it's in the mind, and he has you to carry out that order, which means it's in the heart. So you're doing what he tells you to do. That is just like the devil.

CHAPTER 23

YOUR JOURNEY ALONG THE WAY

While we are on this Christian journey, stay watchful for those that cause divisions in the church and try to put obstacles in your way. Keep away from them. The enemy has them, and they are just like their father the enemy – sneaky and smooth talking, with nice flattery words. They have been deceived and they are in a comfort zone fast asleep.

God wants us to stay in a victory mode and by doing that we must stay in a ready mode in the Word of God. When the enemy comes up against us we can defeat him with the Word of God. The more you meditate on God's Word, the stronger you'll become and the more easily you'll win the victory. You must realize that once you give your life to the Lord, the natural man is still there along with the spiritual man, these two make up the believer, but it's two separate men. We must remember that we can't get rid of the old nature until the death of our body (of our flesh). Therefore the warfare must continue until death. Don't even try to make a fair showing of your flesh. We are to have no confidence in the flesh. When we feed our flesh, we are giving the enemy the right away to have a field day in our life. Yes, in our Christian journey along the way, there are many things you and I will experience that involves the other nature; and if we let the enemy resurrect the old man, it will come back alive and cause much trouble. That's what the enemy is after – that old man so he can use it and that's so sad after we have put it to death.

Come on. Use what it takes to stay on the right path of righteousness. We must starve the flesh and make no provision for it to fulfill the lust thereof. Feed the new man. At first when we were babes, we were fed with the sincere milk of the Word. But we must be fed regularly. The more we feed the new man, the less we have to worry about the old man because he gets weakened down and causes little trouble. We have to keep him dead. If we're not being watchful, the enemy will revive that old man and he will gain strength and give us trouble. Be careful. Don't let the enemy revive that old man, and if you do, you're in trouble.

CHAPTER 24

FALLING BACK TO FORMER HABITS

This accounts for how some Christians who have lived a consecrated spiritual life for years suddenly fall having yielded in an unguarded moment to some former habits of their old nature. I remember our family had a gathering. As I looked around I saw my family on my mother's side. Most of them were all in church, saved, and filled with the Holy Ghost, and as the years rolled by many of them turned lukewarm, some backslid, and some claim something that they used to have but don't have it no more. The enemy, in other words, is having them playing church. Some of their former habits came back on them.

When you're like that, you are messed up. It's not good when you're in that area of life. Again the devil tells you that you are alright as long as you can go to church, get your shout on, do your tongue speaking, and leave when it's time for the Word of God. The enemy has you fooled and thinking you're all right when you are not. The more I see the more I want to get closer and closer to God. The enemy is no joke. Why can't we see what the enemy is doing to us? As I always say, if you don't wake up you're going to lift up your eyes in Hell. There are many saints out there who don't have a shepherd. They go from church to church. When you are like that, you pick up many spirits. Take note! That's not good.

Why would you let the enemy carry you back to your former habits? Shelter yourself under a good shepherd where you can be fed with the Word of God. The enemy's trying to put you in a place where he can steal and destroy you and you're unaware of it because it seems like to you it's okay. I'm telling you. When old former habits are back you're doing something wrong.

We cannot feed both the natures at the same time, and if we want to stay strong in the Lord, you cannot read and study the Word and look at TV at the same time or talk on the telephone and listen to music or hold a conversation. It's one or the other. If we feed one nature, we will starve the other nature. So I'm telling you let us starve the old man. Eat the Word of God so the new man can stay strong. In (Galatians 5:16) it states: *This I say then, Walk in the Spirit, and ye shall not fulfill the lust of the flesh.* As you walk in the Spirit, start amputating. Whatever is hindering your walk with Christ, cut it off. As you walk in the Spirit do some mortification. In (Colossians 3:5) it states *Mortify therefore your members which are upon the earth; fornication, uncleanness, inordinate affection, evil concupiscence, and covetousness, which is idolatry.* All of this is the enemy's junk and we must put it to death. Don't forget there is a limitation, we must lay aside every weight and the sin which doth so easily beset us and let us run with patience the race that is set before us. As we run we have to look to Jesus who is the author and the finisher of our faith.

When the new nature is finally given the right away it will bring forth the fruit of the Spirit. In the Bible (Galatians 5: 22-23) states *But the fruit of the spirit is love, joy, peace, longsuffering, gentleness, goodness, faith, Meekness, temperance: against such there is no law.* This is your journey. Don't let the enemy put a road block in your path or stop you from going forth. He is setting up construction, working on those saints that he has captured. The enemy has a sign up saying "Under construction." You can see by the lifestyle they are living that some people have left God to be under construction by the enemy, giving heed to his voice and letting him tear down their righteousness in Christ Jesus. The enemy sets up a road block. Then he starts to bring all kinds of miserable spirits to dwell in your life and you don't have what you're used to having because he stole your rights in the Lord. The first thing he grabs and pulls is your faith. Then doubt sets in. I'm talking about unbelief. He will have you in a place where you will pull off the fruit of the Spirit of the Lord and he will tell you that you don't need it. These fruit you do need, I'm talking about love, joy, peace, longsuffering, gentleness, goodness, faith, meekness, and temperance. The devil will replace them with what he has to offer, envying, murders, witchcraft, hatred, fornication, adultery, uncleanness, and you name it – everything that is unrighteous. Sometimes we are unaware or sometimes forget who we are in Christ Jesus. Again in (Galatians 5:16) it states: *This I say then, Walk in the spirit, and ye shall not fulfill the lust of the flesh.*

That unwanted spirit that we once had, the one I'm talking about is the one that was familiar with us before we gave our life to Christ Jesus. That's the spirit that knows us. When we are knocked off course by the devil, the doors open for him to bring them back so what he does is set up a road block for him to put a sign up that says, "They are under construction." All these things the enemy will do, but you know one thing? He will bring your familiar spirits back to you along with other spirits that don't know you, and if you don't get delivered from them, they will get to know you along with the ones that knew you at first. When the Lord saves us and delivers us, we became free. We are clean-through the Word of God. As time passes when you don't pray, don't read The Word of God and don't be watchful, that opens the door for the enemy to get a hold on us and put us under his construction of darkness, no light just darkness, for the devil everything goes. He's working hard to stop you from making it into the kingdom of heaven. Again once upon a time he was there, and he's loading up as many as he can to be with him; so don't let yourself be in his number.

You don't have to stay like that. You can get repaired in God's Word. Everything we need is in the Word of God. He told us to keep His commandments and abide in Him, and if we ask anything in His name He will give it to us. The problem with us today is we don't like to obey the Word of God, but we are quick to obey the devil. All those who make it to prayer meeting, keep church doors open, are great workers in the church , and other good things that you do, it's alright that you do these things. You must remember the enemy sees how well you are very faithful to your church, but I'm serving you notice that he doesn't care. He's trying to find out how to get you. See, he comes to church. He whispers in your ear and tells you they need you and you don't need them. That's when he is working on your mind, and all the things you were doing all of a sudden you stop doing them.

No Bible Study, no prayer, and you stop reading The Word of God. Then you start to think about what he has told you. "They need me." That's a door open for him to slide in and set up housekeeping in your life. Do you want to defeat the enemy? Stay in the Word of God. Stay on your post being watchful at all times.

CHAPTER 25

IT'S GOOD TO KNOW

You must recognize that you are a sinner and cannot save yourself, Repent and turn from your sins. All those who have gone to sleep, wake up. Come back to the Lord. God knows that you have backslidden and been filled up with your ways where the enemy spoke to you and tricked you into believing these words *"It's alright to do what God has forbidden."* All God wants you to do is return unto Him. He will not keep His anger forever, for God is merciful and longsuffering, full of love. (Jeremiah 3:14) states *Turn, O backsliding children, said the Lord: for I am married unto you: and I will take you one of a city, and two of a family, and I will bring you to Zion.* God's Word is true. Don't let the enemy fool you.

God will give you a Pastor according to His heart, which shall feed you with knowledge and understanding. I am talking about a Pastor who has been sold out and has his or her mind made up to go all the way with the Lord, who's living

Holy, the one walking upright, and that loves souls. God wants His people to be saved and blessed. God is concerned about you and me. That's why He sent His Son Jesus to pay the price on Calvary. Sin separates us from the love of God. But we don't have to stay in the shape that we are in. We can be changed. Give Jesus a try. Let Him come into your life and save you so you won't be lost.

If you live after the flesh, you are going to die: if you live through the Spirit, there are things you have to let go. And the enemy doesn't want you to let it go. He wants you to hold on to it, and if you do you won't make it in when Jesus comes back. He knows that, that's why he is behind you every step you take in life. We as believers are made son and heir; that means daughter too. Since we are, we have received the Spirit of adoption we can go to God in prayer. We cry Abba Father. We tell him all about our problems. The Spirit itself beareth witness with our spirit, that we are the children of God. If we are children, then heirs; heirs of God, and joint heirs with Christ; If so be that we suffer with Him, that we may be also glorified together. We who are in Christ Jesus, the enemy has nothing on us. He's just waiting for a door to open up so he can slip in.

I have told you about the enemy. Now I'm going to describe his characteristics; he's a liar from the beginning who misled the human race, a murderer, he murdered the whole human race in that all are dead in trespasses and sin, the accuser, the hinderer, the tempter, the seducer of saints and most of all the rebellious. The enemy – He is the one that's going to go forth to open war against Christ and the saints. Really he is crazy for messing with Christ. And it won't be long. The day is coming when the enemy will be cast into a lake of fire. What a day that will be for him.

See, it's good to know these things. One thing you and I don't know is the time and the hour when Jesus will be here. We must get ready and stay ready at all times. Don't let the enemy speak to you and tell you that Jesus is not coming or He changed His mind. If anything the enemy is trying to change your mind about salvation and living for Jesus Christ. Somebody asked a question "Whose side are you on?" Then somebody answered and said "I'm on the Lord's side." So we can say, "Devil, I'm on the Lord's side. Let nobody tell you something different."

Why put off today and wait until tomorrow to give your life to Christ? Now is the day of salvation. The enemy tells us lies for years and years and he's still telling lies. He has not stopped doing what he does and that's deceiving people over and over again. When you find yourself falling for what he does you are giving him victory and that's what he wants. All he does is make a fool out of you and then laughs at you. Many people today let the enemy get over on them. I have heard some say it's the blessing from the Lord. They get the devil's blessing mixed up with The Lord's blessing. Just like in the church praises go up from different ones. Some are being blessed and some the enemy is using them to disrupt the service. And when he finishes with whatever he uses them for, he leaves them feeling shame. That's the way it is – sin and shame. The enemy will make you cover up your wrong doing and tell you it's okay and what you did wasn't wrong. But when you find yourself in a jam or a mess – what I mean is when it comes to the light then he will have you trying to cover it up or trying to fix it. Then it's too late.

That's what happened to David in the Bible. David rose from off his bed and walked upon the roof of the king's house, and from the roof he saw a woman washing herself and she was very beautiful to look upon. He sent and inquired after the woman. They told him her name and that she was another man's wife, and they gave him the woman whose husband was Uriah the Hittite. It was an "I don't care thing" going on and that's the way the enemy operates. So David sent for her and he lay with her. That few seconds of pleasure led to something else out of hand. That's what the enemy will do. She conceived and sent and told David, "I am with child." Now David had to find a way of covering his tracks. He sent to Joab and told him to send him Uriah. Uriah came in. David asked him questions about Joab, the people and the war. Most likely Uriah gave an answer that David wanted to hear so David told him, "You can go home to your wife." The Lord was in the plan. Uriah didn't go home and it was told to David that he slept at the door at the king's house with all of the servants. David told Uriah "Your journey away from home was long. Why didn't you go to your house?" Uriah said unto David, "The ark, and Israel and Judah, abide in the tents; and my lord Joab, and the servants of my lord, are encamped in the open fields;" Uriah said, "Shall I go home to eat, drink and lie with my wife?" he said "as thou livest, and as thou soul liveth, I will not do this thing."

For David that was plan number one. Now plan number two was to make Uriah drunk so he could go home, but he didn't go home. He lay on the bed with the servants of his lord. David came up with plan number three. He wrote a letter to Joab and sent it by the hand of Uriah. In that letter to Joab were instructions to set Uriah in the hottest battle "put him in the front, then you withdraw yourself from him so he will be struck down and die." The order was carried out, Uriah and others got killed so David took Uriah's wife to be his wife. But what I am saying is that's what the enemy does – have you doing wrong on top of wrong and if you don't correct that, you have to keep on doing wrong and it seems like there is no end until you come clean by turning it over to the Lord. Covering up wrong is wrong. God sees all things. You will get a visitation from God. That's what happened to David. What David did displeased the Lord. God sent Nathan the Prophet and rebuked David. The child that Bathsheba bare, the Lord struck with sickness. David fasted and prayed. He lay all night upon the earth. The child died.

We must remember David was a king. The Lord said that he would raise up evil against him right out of his house, and his wives would be taken and given to his neighbor. The Lord told David you did yours in secret but I will do this thing before all Israel, and before the sun. At that time they lived under the law, and we are under grace. So all you that have a title, make sure you are not letting the enemy cover you up. God sees and He knows.

Sometime I wonder why we go that way before we get the picture. The enemy doesn't care whether we get the picture or not. He's on a mission for Hell and he's trying to gather all that he can to be miserable with him. There is nothing in Hell but torment forever and ever, why you want to go there when God sent His Son to pay the price so you and I could have everlasting life? God was so concerned about us whom He made in His image after His likeness that He sent His Son to deal with sin. God sees what the enemy is doing to us. God loves us so much He made a way for you and I. God has the whole world in His hand. All in the Bible we see how the enemy operates. He's all in our way with his demon spirits. He's not going to stop messing with us. That's his job; the only occupation he has.

We know someone who can and will put him out of business forever. Hold on and stay committed to God's unchanging hand. Keep yielding to God in the midst of the storm. Make your mind up and sell out to Jesus and don't let the devil separate you from God's love. If you give the enemy a chance to slide in, you are in trouble.

Many born again believers have let the devil slide into their lives unawares and when they notice it, it's too late. Just don't be no fool like the foolish virgins. I call them the last minute Christians who feel like I can do my thing and still make it in. Not so. The enemy has many thinking that they can go to heaven at the last minute. If that's the case, what happened to him? Why is he not there? You read in the early part of my book what happened to him. He outsmarted himself and got thrown out. Well his plans didn't work.

The enemy doesn't want us to stay in the Word of God because we will find him out. Anyway God wants us to study to show ourselves approved unto God, workmen that needeth not to be ashamed, righty dividing the word of truth.

Stay in the Word of God so you have what it takes to war with the enemy. He doesn't want none of us to learn the Word of God. The devil knows when he comes up against us and by us reading the Word of God and applying it to our life daily we have something to fight him with. That's why he doesn't want us to study the Word. It's something how he aims for the ones who are saved and living for the Lord. We were taken out of his hands. He's trying to get us back. It's something how he plans up many things to get us. As long as we stay in the Word and don't yield our members as instruments of unrighteousness unto sin, we will be on safe grounds because we'll be yielding our instrument of righteousness unto God by saying no to our enemy.

In (Ephesians 4:27) it states: *Neither give place to the devil.* We can't let him have an opportunity to do or say what he wants in our life. God's got the say so in our life. We belong to the Lord. The devil knows. That's why he's trying every attempt to get us in a place so he can grab us to himself. No matter what, stay with the Lord and go through the pain, the hardship, and the suffering. God's going to bring us out with victory. He sees and knows what we can bear. In due season, God will lift us up. Stay humble unto the Lord and obey Him.

CHAPTER 26

THE GARBAGE DUMP

The promises of God are in Jesus Christ. In (1 John 3:8) the Bible states: *He that committeth sin is of the devil; for the devil sinneth from the beginning. For this purpose the Son of God was manifested, that he might destroy the works of the devil.* That's why the Son of God appeared – for this purpose that He might destroy the works of the enemy.

All the damage that the enemy caused in your life, Jesus came on the scene to bail you out. Stay alert. The devil is still our enemy, or you can vice or versa it, our enemy is still the devil. We need to stay in The Word of God at all times. Jesus doesn't give up on us. We get inpatient and give up on Him. Wait on God. Stop collecting garbage from the enemy. He's like the city dump. Only one thing he doesn't do is pick up. He delivers. Could you picture in your mind all the stuff that the city dump has, and that's a lot because they pick-up. Think of all the garbage the enemy has. Think of all of that unrighteousness that he gives to his workers to deliver so they can dump some more inside the lukewarm Christians and deliver and dump on God's people who are saved and doing a work for Christ.

That's why your mind shouldn't be idle, because the enemy will come along and dump garbage in your mind; and if you don't rebuke it right away, it will go to the heart and take root. He will use all these carnal things to trap you if he can. He will try to get you up into your lifestyle doing the things you used to do before you came to Christ if you're not reading the Word of God like you should, coming to Bible study, praying and fasting. Because the enemy knows that if you don't find out what God's Word says you will always be the one he dumps his garbage not on but in you. When he dumps his garbage on you, you will be dirty on the outside, but in you, you will be messed up on the inside – a collector for the enemy and he loves that.

Jesus made it possible that you can defeat the devil in your life and that is through the Word of God. I have a question for you. What are you doing with the Word of God? I know some will say *I read the Word*. Some will say *it's at home collecting dust*, and some will say *I apply the Word of God to my life*. Others will say *the Word of God is not working for me*. You can read, apply and doubt, but the Word of God makes a change in your life. The Word of God has life. The Word of God is alive. If you allow the Word to get in you, a change will take place in your life. The only way things will happen in our life with the Word is we have to do what the Bible says. (James 1:22) states *Be ye doers of the word, and not hearers only deceiving your own selves.* So the Word of God is telling us to do what the Word says do. Let us hear the Word and do the Word. If anyone doesn't do what the Word says do, you are deceiving yourselves.

It's time to come up to the Word. The Word is not coming down to you. We who have been in Christ Jesus for years and years – we haven't made it yet. We have to make sure we stay on the right road and don't get off, don't turn around, don't short cut, don't choose or pick in the Word of God. Eat all of the Word of God. God told Ezekiel to eat the Word and he opened his mouth and he did eat the Word. He filled his bowels with the Word and Ezekiel said in his mouth the Word was as honey for sweetness. By Ezekiel eating the Word of God, he was used by God to speak the Word to the dry bones. Which had no life in them, He spoke life to them and caused God's Spirit to breathe life in them. By prophesying unto the wind Ezekiel told the wind, *Thus saith the Lord God; Come from the four winds, O breath, and breathe upon these slain, that they may live.* God caused flesh to come upon them. The Word of God is powerful and full of life. The Word lives. We have the best for our enemy when he comes to keep knocking at our door. Eat the Word so you can put the Word on him. Everything is going down but the Word of God. The Word is tight but it's right, and will keep you going right. The Lord told Ezekiel these bones are the whole house of Israel: and these are the words that they are saying, *that their bones are all dried, and their hope is lost: they felt like that they were cut off for their parts.*

We are like them – don't want to obey the Lord, but playing around with the enemy. The devil will bring you down to his dump and fill you with his garbage and after he fills you up, it takes God to unload you by delivering you of all that junk that the devil has dumped in you. The Lord builds you back and puts life back into you. We are the ones that mess up, here comes God to strengthen and restore us back. Don't you think God gets tired of us messing up and we have His Word? We are too lazy to get into the Word of God. We find ourselves doing something else. We all are guilty for that, so don't try to throw it off on nobody. Let's make this one personal – point our finger at ourselves. We have something to pray about. It's me Lord that needs help. And we can say Lord when you finish with me then I will be able to help somebody else. Remember David in Psalms 51, he asked God to *restore the joy of thy salvation and uphold me with thy free spirit.* Then he went on to say *then will I teach transgressors thy ways:* See when you are bound up you can't help nobody. You need help yourself. David got it right and we need to get it right with God and get it right with our sisters and brothers in Christ, which the enemy doesn't want us to do that. He is mad with God and he wants us to be mad with one another. Also he wants us to disobey God.

I got a question to ask, whose side are you on? My answer, I'm on the Lord's side and I am like Joshua, as for me and my house we will serve the Lord. God's been too good to me for me to keep messing up on him. There could be a time when you go forth to mess up that the Lord could come, and you will miss out on going back with Him when He comes. Joshua told them to *put away your strange gods that you have among you, and incline your heart unto the Lord God of Israel.* The enemy has us carrying around strange gods. It doesn't have to be a statue, anything you love more than God can be your gods.

I have had conversations with many that say they are born-again Christians. They told me all the good things God has done for them in their life. Yet they left God and don't even want to come back. They're living in the comfortable zone. They come to church and can talk about how The Lord is blessing them and how they witness to others about the goodness of Jesus and what He can do for them; But when it comes down to giving their life to the Lord and living a holy life, they are not for that. They feel like they're okay. The enemy has them fooled sitting right in church reaping all the good blessings from God. The Bible says *let the wheat and the tares grow together.* What's so sad is all those people who go to church and claiming that they are saved or born-again Christians not living according to The Word of God. That's dangerous, and you know what the very sad part about that is? Going to Hell from the house which we call the church. I wonder what it takes for people like that. The devil's really got them and they think they're okay but not so. They are living their lifestyle in their own world.

I have seen in my life times where the enemy has taken some of the Christians who have once been saved and running for Jesus for a long time, done cooled off, not been watchful, playing around, the devil telling them you got time. But in the long run they got fooled by the enemy. The enemy has taken them and has put them under his construction, and is bringing a lot of his miserable spirits into their life. Some of those spirits know them and the ones that don't know him or her, those are the one's that are new. Yes, under construction those evil spirits tearing down everything that they once built up in their life when they gave their life to Christ and when they were seeking Christ. The devil will tamper with everything you got until he destroys you. The fruit of righteousness he will strip off you little by little. He will let you keep some. You go to church, you sing songs like everybody else. He will have you in a comfortable zone where you lost your joy, your love went cold, you don't have peace, you can't sleep at night, you have no faith, you stopped believing God, your temper is all messed up, and the devil has you mad with everybody.

There are many today who are just not going to church because they say the church which is the building where people go to worship, has been turned into an asking for money theme. They tell me that they see nothing that the church is doing – not even building a church. The Church is supposed to be about winning souls to Christ, visitation of the sick, and clothing and feeding the people who don't have. The enemy changed all of that into loving to raise money to help themselves in their pleasure of life. What about the souls that the Lord wants us to win for Him? Today many souls go from church to church looking for a place to worship and to hear the Word of God. Many churches have been turned over into a place of entertainment. They have money lines of prosperity, and if you don't have a large amount of money they don't want to be bothered with you or pronounce that a blessing is coming your way. What about salvation? God is concerned about the whole person. It's in His Word (3 John 1-2) states; *Beloved, I wish above all things that thou mayest prosper and be in health, even as thy soul prospereth.* Yet and still, they will quote "Whoever's giving other than what I am asking for, put it over there in that basket." God is not pleased with that. Remember in the Bible, the rich men casting their gifts into the treasury and Jesus saw the poor widow casting in thither two mites. In (Luke 21:3-4) it states: *And he said, Of a truth I say unto you, that this poor widow hath cast in more than they all: For all these have of their abundance cast in unto the offerings of God: but she of her penury hath cast in all the living that she had.* So it doesn't matter how many money lines these churches have. The ones that they tell to put their money over into that basket those are the ones that are blessed because they are giving from the heart.

God looks at the heart and how you giving, and that's from the heart. The devil has everything backwards and twisted up. A lot of preachers are letting the enemy use them. They think they're in the service of the Lord but a lot of things the enemy has them doing, and it's not of the Lord. We as preachers need to go back to the old time way. I am talking about holiness, living the Bible way. God doesn't want none of us to be lost. The Word of God is the truth, and the truth is that God always causes you to triumph in Christ Jesus. So if you are not triumphing, you need to get in Christ Jesus! It is worth the effort to triumph. That means you have the right to become the Righteousness of God in Christ Jesus. You have His Righteousness! Don't let the enemy ever tell you that you are not worthy again, because the Bible says, Jesus Christ bestowed His righteous-ness on you when you received Him as Savior. The Righteousness of God, He is for us. Taking care of us and He is watching over us.

Look, if the churches get right everything else falls in place. First it starts with the leaders, then goes down to the members. You can't let the enemy rule the church. You can't let the people in the church do whatever they want to do. Some saints have their cliques in the corner. They come to church when the Pastor is there and when the Pastor is not there they don't come, and those that do come don't want to listen to the next person who the Pastor put in charge. Something's wrong with that picture, and the devil has a hold on them. I am quite sure that the devil done told them you don't have to listen; you are grown; you can choose the way you want. That's a lie he done told them because God gives leaders over His people. The enemy wants to be your leader. That's why he's there disturbing things. He's on a rampage killing many young people, just shooting them down. We are living in perilous times where the enemy has people loving themselves and being lovers of pleasure more than God. Many marriages in the churches and outside the churches have been broken up because of the enemy. He doesn't like anything that the Lord honors. All Satan likes is the opposite. He tells them after being married so many years – and some three years or less than a year – he speaks and tells him or her you don't have to be married or it's better to shack up. You'll get along better. He's having them running from responsibility and is making them get deeper into something that they can't get out of.

That's just like satan. Trying to reverse everything and make it the opposite of what God says. The Lord knows what our enemy is all about that's why The Lord gave us His word so we can search the Word of God. In (John 5:39) it states: *Search the scriptures; for in them ye think ye have eternal life: and they are they which testify of me.* If you are in Christ Jesus, only He can make a marriage; and when a saint of God wants a divorce from their husband or wife, somebody has stepped outside of Christ and the enemy has flesh operating in sin. In life, as I see the times we are living in, I search myself daily. I don't want to be lost. Things are not going to get any better. Satan is on a rampage trying to keep us blind so we don't recognize God when He is in our midst. God is everywhere.

CHAPTER 27

THE DEVIL IS NOT YOUR GOD

W e have come too far to turn around to go back into the world. Yes, at times we get really tired along the way and we want to sit down and rest a little while. Make sure your thinking is right with God. I believe God wants us to grasp where we are at this point. The devil is not your God. God wants us to reach out and receive everything He has to give us for this journey. If we reach out and accept God's offer, we will grow into a relationship with Him no matter what it costs us, or we can let the enemy fool us and go back into his arms.

I don't know about you, but I don't want to go back into the arms of Satan. I came too far to turn back now and for my soul to be lost. Why should I when I have already learned to understand that with God all things are possible and I can live in the present tense. I can walk in the newness of life of what He has for me everyday. The enemy's trick is to have us to stop right in the middle of the race. He doesn't want any of us to endure or finish, nor make it into the Kingdom of heaven. The enemy delights in seeing us fall down or pull out of the race that is set before us. We have to remember that we are on the winning side, so let us stay in the race and finish until the end, the same shall be saved.

Commit yourselves unto the Lord all the way with a true relationship with Him. Give Him your whole heart. What The Lord tells you, do it with joy. Occupy time until Jesus comes back for you. Don't neglect this great opportunity of salvation and if you miss out, in Hell you're going to lift up your eyes. Hell is real, in the Bible, this rich man dressed in purple and fine linen and fared sumptuously every day, he could have helped Lazarus (the beggar), but his mind was on himself and he was not even thinking about God and what was going to happen to him when he leaves this life. Anyway he died without salvation, and in Hell he lifted up his eyes being tormented. He cried out for help, for comfort, just like the beggar wanted some food to eat from the rich man and he didn't want to be bothered by helping Lazarus (the beggar).

So this rich man sent a message from Hell "Father Abraham" have mercy on me, and asked him to send Lazarus (the beggar) to dip the tip of his finger in water and cool his tongue, and he said he was tormented. Abraham said "son remember in your lifetime you received good things and Lazarus (the beggar) evil things. He went on to tell him between where you are and where I am there is a big gulf fixed. They who want to help you out can't pass from here to you, neither you from there to here. Now the rich man wanted to pray to him that he would send someone to his father's house to warn his five brethren about Hell the place of torment. Abraham said unto him that they have Moses and the prophets. Let them hear them.

That rich man thought if one came from the dead they would repent. Abraham told him if they don't hear Moses and the Prophets, how in the world would they be persuaded though one rose from the dead? I hope you are planning on going to heaven. Don't get yourselves twisted up with the enemy. If you do, that's bad news forever and ever.

For we have spent enough of our past lifetime with the devil, when we walked in licentiousness, lusts, drunkenness, revelries, partying and drinking harming our bodies among other things I didn't mention. We as Christians should live with an attitude of serious prayer and getting closer and closer to God. Learn how to endure trials with the right attitude. Go through your trails and your suffering for Christ; and if you do, it shows that you really are following Jesus and that we suffer because we are identified with Him.

Our adversary the devil, our enemy is walking around hunting for souls. While he is hunting, we should be clear headed and in a watchful state. He already has permission from God to bother us. He has access to you. He knows your feelings and your propensities and informs himself of all your circumstances; you must remember only God can know more and do more then satan. Our cares must be cast upon God.

In (1 Peter 5:8) the Bible states: *Be sober, be vigilant; because your adversary the devil, as a roaring lion, walketh about, seeking whom he may devour.* Look at this. As Christians we have satan as a lion who may roar but who has been defeated at the cross. Yes, the sound of his roar comes with his deceptive lies aiming to devour souls and rob Christians of their effectiveness in Christ Jesus.

Our enemy comes against us like a roaring lion. He's loud and full of intimidation. The enemy roars through persecution, strong temptation, blasphemies and accusations against God. Satan's goal is to seek whom he may devour. He can never be content till he sees us as a believer in Christ Jesus devoured. Our enemy would rend us in pieces, and break our bones and utterly destroy us if he could. As long as we are in Christ Jesus, we can resist him, his lies, threats and intimidation, and stay fast in the faith. Every time you see our enemy being very active, pray more and more. On that test, he will give up because he sees that it's driving you to Christ. We are all in this together because we all have an enemy to fight. So keep on fighting him with the Word of God.

CHAPTER 28

FLEE FROM EVILS

There are a lot of things that the enemy has out, but we must flee from them. In the world today people love money and would do anything to get it. We who are in the world but not of the world shouldn't get caught up into that. The Word of God has everything we need when we come across something that's trying to take us away from God.

In (1 Timothy 6:10) it states: *For the love of money is the root of all evil: which while some coveted after, they have erred from the faith, and pierced themselves through with many sorrows.* See it's evil if you love money. It takes root in your life and grows, causes you to do all kinds of evil things a lot of Christian in the church have failed because the enemy has blinded their minds and they went into error and that's happening today. The devil has them loving money rather than loving God. You know what they are doing – stealing the church money. Not only from the church but from God. In (Malachi 3:8) it states: *Will a man rod God? Yet ye have robbed me. But ye say, when in have we robbed thee? In tithes and offerings.* The enemy doesn't want us to obey the Word of God. He wants us to be just like him. Many today have holes in their pockets for not paying their tithes and giving their offering in God's house. Not only that – they're feeling unhappy, but the enemy had a hold on them. They couldn't help it at that time. We must flee from evil. The enemy tells them, "you can get away with it; nobody knows." See how he does his cover-up.

The Bible in (1 timothy 6:11) states: *But thou O man of God, flee these things; and follow after righteousness, godliness, faith, love, patience, meekness.* We are in warfare with our enemy. Don't let him take you. Let him know who you are standing for. I'm on the Lord's side. I'm fighting the good fight of faith, laying hold of eternal life. God's been good to us all and He loves us. Flee from the things that will make you turn your back on God. Not only that, you'll miss out in making it into the Kingdom of heaven.

The enemy is our adversary, our foe, who doesn't like us, who hates us because we love The Lord. He's seeking to harm us, to kill us, and to destroy us. There's no good thing in satan; He has revealed himself as such throughout history by seeking to hurt men and women, leading them away from God. Our enemy is on his post. Why can't we be on our post steadfast un-moveable, always abounding in the work of the Lord, knowing that our labor will not be in vain in the Lord? Let us hold on to God no matter what. When the storms of life hit you, just hold on to God. He sees and he knows all about it. Don't you ever think the devil is going to lift off you. He's going to work you and make your life miserable until Jesus comes back to get us. The Lord wants us to commit ourselves to His will. That includes our mind, body, really our life totally to him.

Don't depend on the arms of flesh. It will fail you. In order to grow in the Lord, it will take much prayer, fasting and studying the Word of God to show ourselves approved unto God. The Lord inspired man to write just what we need to get through this battle; and you know the battle is not ours, it is the Lord's. Daily, we need to submit ourselves to Christ by learning and obeying the Word of God. The next time the devil comes, we should have ourselves charged up with the Word on the inside of us ready to put him in his place.

CHAPTER 29

START TODAY

Make room for Jesus today. Don't be like the world. Many people in this life used to know the Lord. They would go to church with their family. Somehow, when things began to look good from their point of view and when blessings started flowing, they forgot that God existed and they went after the blessing. In other words the enemy closed their eyes on the One who blessed them and made them open their eyes to him and give him the credit. The devil didn't do nothing but make a mess as always.

That's what the enemy did to the Israelites. God delivered them out of the land of Egypt and while they were in the wilderness their leader, Moses was up there with God getting the Word for them. They couldn't wait for him to return. They were saying it was taking Moses too long. Some said "Maybe he's not going to return." They said, "We need us a leader to lead us." So Aaron told them to take off the gold then he melted it down and made them a golden calf.

The devil had them on one accord doing the wrong thing and gave the calf the credit for what God had done for them. So much is going on in the world and nothing's changed; but the enemy has made a change in the people. The Word of God is the same yesterday, today, and forever. We see God and moral candidates are not accepted, while ethics and character has been thrown away. Christianity, once the backbone of the U.S. now is in the minority. I know you have a question – Why? The enemy has them having their own way when it comes down to God. He hates God and he wants the people to hate God also.

The devil has made the people put Jesus out. When the devil has his say so or has his hands in his plans he causes damage. There's no room for God in the court house any more, no upholding moral laws in constitution. When God says things are illegal, satan makes it legal. Think about it. Same sex marriage, abortion, and divorce for any reason. What about the vows that were taken? There are more divorces in the churches today than ever before in my lifetime. It's the enemy's seeds of wrongness. He's on the war path in taking God out of everything. One of the biggest problems is when he used that woman and others to sign that petition to take prayer out of school. The enemy replaced prayer with guns, drugs, and students being sexually attacked by teachers who have a sex problem.

There's no discipline what so ever. We are close to the endtime where some churches are not what they used to be when souls were being saved, healed, blessed and set free. Many churches have turned into entertainment centers where many want to feel good with just music and dancing. It's not the Sunday service anymore, it's the Sunday circus. The devil has some of the ones who know God in a relaxed mode not even caring to hear the Word of God like they used to. The devil speaks to them and tells them "You've been in church long enough. Try to master it.

Don't let nobody come and tell you anything." The enemy speaks and tells you that you got it made. He will show you his devilish plans and he will have you to fall for it. I remember, I went out to help this church about 25 years ago. The deacon of that church heard me preach one time, and he came to me and told me "Don't you come into our church to change nothing." I was not changing anything, but my preaching the Word of God was correcting him and he didn't want to take it.

One of the preachers I know got together with me and we had a revival at that church and invited all the members that belong to that church. Five nights of revival and the Lord blessed every night. The devil jumped into the deacon and he told me to leave his church family and his family alone, and he told me they had other things to do than to come to that meeting because it's too much for them. Satan himself knows if they all get free he won't have them anymore. The enemy wants your soul to go to Hell with him. He's not interested in you.

As the months went by while I was there at that church, I had a one on one with that deacon. He called himself lecturing me because I preached about will we continue to rob God. He picked up his Bible, and we had a talk out of (Malachi 3: 8-10) where it states: *Will a man rob God? Yet ye have robbed me. But ye say, Wherein have we robbed thee? In tithes and offerings. Ye are cursed with a curse: for ye have robbed me, even this whole nation. Bring ye all the tithes into the storehouse, that there may be meat in my house, and prove me now herewith, saith the Lord of hosts, if I will not open you the windows of heaven, and pour you out a blessing, that there shall not be room enough to receive it.*

He read the same Scripture and he told me he is not robbing God. That's his money that he worked hard for, and not only that, he said this scripture is for the Old Testament people and it's not for us today. I told him The Word of God from Genesis to Revelation is for us today. He said, "I put money in church" and I asked him "Are you giving God what belongs to Him?" He kept saying "I put money in church. That's the way I feel." and he walks around with his big fat cigar in his mouth right in church with no shame or respect. The enemy had told him to go against me. The devil knew if I stayed there somebody would get delivered, and he went to his Pastor and told the Pastor that they didn't have any problems until I came in and all these revival services didn't make sense. It tired the people out.

All the things the Pastor asked me to do to help him and the church had faded away. He came to me and said to lighten up on the deacon and don't be preaching too hard. He does give money in the church, and not to have too many services so the people wouldn't get tired. The Church, the Deacon and the Pastor needed to be delivered. The Pastor didn't want preaching of salvation in the church so I told the Pastor of that church I'm going back to my home church. He claimed he hated to see me go. Three to four weeks later I left and went back home to my church before I lost what I had in Christ.

When you are around weak people, if you are not careful you will get weak. See I'm from a Church that believes in the Word of God, fasting, praying, and seeking God, tarrying, and getting what you want from God. There were all kinds of spirits up in that church. The usher, when she's marching the choir in has a mouth full of snuff, and that's a habit and weight which she thinks is okay when it's not okay. I met some very nice people in that church. They just need Jesus. The deacon didn't want to be delivered and he didn't want them to be delivered. The Pastor obeyed the deacon. What kind of mess is that? That's what's going on today in this world and the enemy plays a very important part in that. Yes, he has his hands in anything unrighteous. He's all for it.

CHAPTER 30

THE CHURCHES TODAY

People don't worship in the churches like they used to. Some come in and leave out the same way that they entered. Many come to church just to be coming. Some come there just looking around; while others don't want to be there, but they come to let people know they were in church. Others don't know why they are there. You have some who know why they are there – to worship God. You have some there holding their child while a seat is empty next to them. They could put that child down and give God some praise. Many are clock watchers. When the Lord wants to bless His people, the devil has them sitting on God.

The Lord wants to move, but there are too many spirits, and some people sit and are put to sleep by the enemy. There are many other things that go on in the churches while service is going on. Saints today have that *I can't help it spirit.* They like to do things their way and get upset if you correct them, especially the ones in the church that have a position. They will get upset with the Pastor and make a smart remark to someone else, "I'm grown I don't have to answer no one but myself." Those are the ones that need to seek the Lord because they are on dangerous ground speaking against the leader. We see what happened to Moses' sister, Miriam. Her mouth got her in trouble.

The Lord came down in the pillar of the cloud, and stood in the door of the tabernacle, and The Lord called Aaron and Miriam. The anger of the Lord was kindled against them and he departed. Because of what she did The Lord put leprosy on her. The devil had them being smart mouth to their Pastor. There are many in the church today with that attitude spirit. Watch yourselves. Something worse will happen to you.

There are so many that come to church just to talk on their cell phones or be in the back seat having fun texting. I could imagine if all the people that come to church get with one accord in the Lord and give Him what's due to Him, the Holy Ghost will have the right away, saints will be getting their blessing and their mind will be conditioned to hear the Word of God. But the people yield to the spirit of the devil and give him victory. We got to put our time in, get all that you can and can all that you can get. The devil doesn't have any reason to have the right away in our churches today. Really it points back to us as leaders because we are the head.

Many leaders today let anything go on in their church because that's how they get their money. What about putting your trust in God? What about praying? It's the enemy that wants to take over. Maybe they don't see that's the devil spirit working in these people in the church.

Take a stand. Let nothing come in and control your place of worship and have no one there who doesn't want to listen to you. Unruly people need to be trained. There's a lot to write about the enemy. He's out there. God doesn't want any of us to go to "HELL." In (Romans 3:11) it states: *There is none that understandeth, there is none that seeketh after God.* Man does not seek after God, but in His love, God seeks man so that he will not go to Hell. You cannot go to heaven by church membership or good works, only through the blood. Don't let the enemy fool you. The enemy is the wrong one in control. Your life and my life were out of control and we were not pleasing in the eyes of God. But praise His name! He allowed us a new beginning by sending His Son Jesus Christ down to die for us. We have a new direction after we have received Jesus Christ as Lord and Savior in our life. It's no more living a worldly life. It's no more obeying what the flesh tells us to do under the instruction and the direction of our enemy. Now it is the will and the Word of God that we obey. We are saved now and have a new life in Christ Jesus. All we have to do is come to Jesus. He will in no wise cast us out. He loves us with an unconditional love and is concerned about where we're going to spend eternal life.

The Bible in (Romans 10:13) states: *For whosoever shall call upon the name of the Lord shall be saved.* He who believes in the Son has everlasting life: and he who does not believe in the Son shall not see life, but the wrath of God abides on him.

Read your Bible daily and obey God's Word. Seek God through prayer with praises and thanksgiving, stay in church and fellowship with other Christians who are living Holy, and tell others about Jesus in your words about your life. Be watchful and don't let the enemy creep into your life.

I pray that this book has helped you in many ways. Our enemy is on the war path trying to block and stop us from living for the Lord. And he doesn't want us to go back with Jesus when He comes back to rapture His Church. Let us make the enemy what he already is – a liar and the father of lies. Speak the Word of God to him and let him know who rules in your life; tell him that he can't have you for you are a child of the King. The only way you can do that is to get into the Word. The Word can't get into you until you get into the Word. There is power in the Word of God and once the Word is in you, the Word will take control of your life.

Those who are not saved, give your life to Christ right now. God made it possible and has a perfect plan for our lives. I'm glad He included me in His plan. If He didn't, we would be lost forever and ever. So tell Christ to come into your life and make Him Lord and Savior. We don't belong to ourselves. Yes we live in this body but once we give our body to the Lord, it's the temple of God. So how're you treating the temple of God? Is the enemy controlling it? God is looking for His people to be dedicated to His Son Jesus in true devotion unto Him, putting everything to death that belongs to the enemy because those things are dishonoring God. If you are not saved, you are not the temple of God. But you can be if you make up your mind right now. He will save you by His grace. God is doing great things today in many lives and I'm so glad He included me. We gave the enemy a chance and he messed us up. Now the question right now is, will you give Jesus the right away in your life? If so, say this prayer below.

Dear Lord Jesus, before reading this book I didn't know I was headed for destruction and that the enemy was ruling my life. I thank you God for sending your Son, Jesus Christ to die on the cross for my sins. I'm sorry for the wrong things that I have done and I'm asking you to forgive me. Right now I'm receiving you into my heart as Savior and Lord. I believe Your promise to make me a child of God. I trust You to give me strength day by day to live for You.

In Your Name Jesus I pray, Amen

About The Author

Pastor Annie Anderson was born in Henderson, North Carolina, the third child of 11 children in the family. She went to Ashworth High School in Atlanta, Georgia where she attended all courses and graduated.

In November 1975, she accepted Jesus as Lord and Savior in her life. She stayed on her knees and tarried until she received the gift of the Holy Spirit. She was called into the ministry in 1978 by God, ordained an evangelist, went to Evangelist Bible Institute and School of Theology under the late Dr. Nathaniel L. Screven Sr., where she received her Bachelor of Theology. She continued her Biblical Education course and received a certificate in Pastoral Theology and a certificate in Biblical Psychology with a focus on the study of activities of the mind.

On November 2, 1997 she was installed as Assistant Pastor at her church. A soul winner for Christ, her life drew her family and many others to Christ. While out in the field working for Christ she did revivals, visited the sick in the hospital, ministered at nursery homes, and worked at feeding the hungry and home visitation. Through her ministry, souls came to Christ and many were blessed. The Lord called her many years ago. He saw that she has a passion for souls. In the year 2011, she said yes to her calling. Her words that she uses while she is ministering or talking are "Picture this. It's all about Jesus." She is now the founder of True Vine Deliverance Ministries Church. This is her first book.

Order Information

You can order additional book copies of
THE ENEMY or contact the author to come to
speak at your meeting, conference and events by
contacting the author through email at
andersonannie14@yahoo.com
montaguelee@gmail.com

You can also order books for $15.00 plus
$3.50 shipping and handling. To order contact
the author by email or by calling (908) 343-9599

Or send check or money order to:
Annie Anderson
P.O. Box 2698
Elizabeth, New Jersey 07208

Also available at Amazon.com
Also available on Kindle

CPSIA information can be obtained
at www.ICGtesting.com
Printed in the USA
FSOW04n1234100616
21392FS

9 780996 383318